Connections Remembered:

African Origins of Humanity and Civilization

The Impact of Historical Memory on Black Identity

By

Lindiwe S. Lester and Sondai K. Lester

Connections Remembered: The African Origins of Humanity and Civilization

ISBN number: 978-1-7344826-0-7

Library of Congress Cataloguing-in-Publication Data

Lester, Lindiwe Stovall and Lester, Sondai Kibwe

Connections Remembered: African Origins of Humanity and Civilization, The Impact of Historical Memory on Black Identity

1. African History
2. Rites of Passage
3. African American Child Development
4. African-Centered Education
5. African American Education
6. African American History

CONTENTS

Dedication

West African Adinkra symbol,

Nsoroma

(meaning: Their illumination is a reflection of God)

Dedicated to our children, Tarik and Noni (and son-in-love George Olayinka), grandsons Jide and Zaire, and all of Africa's children worldwide. We dedicate these pages to you—trusting our and succeeding generations' endeavors help pave a way for you to know and celebrate your Black selves fully and unashamedly, then, go forth unleashing that fullness to change the world.

Preface

A Matter of Racial Memory

By Lindiwe and Sondai

"Where does your identity come from? Your memory, of course."

– Neil deGrasse Tyson

W hy have we updated **Connections Remembered** 20 years since we first published it? Simply put: As a people, we still have a long way to go, and we want to be a part of that continuing journey. We feel compelled to use our voices to ensure *our* history is neither forgotten nor erased. This book is a reminder that history is foundational for educating Black children and for strengthening our communities.

In that same vein, Sondai published *Who Dropped the Ball on Our Kids?* in 2019. The book is unwavering in asserting that Black students' sense of self is linked to the American educational process. There's little chance of Black children, educated in America, escaping acute and persistent assaults on their racial identity early in their development. It is woven into the design of their schooling. Writes Sondai:

> *American institutions, both religious and secular, function as essential agents of socialization into a deeply engrained system of injustice and Black second-class status…A primary role of America's social institutions is to imbed in the minds of the oppressor and the oppressed the 'naturalness' and inescapability of each group's social status.* P. 13 and 14

This revision of ***Connections Remembered*** reinforces the power of education, specifically history, to shape identity. A historically accurate lens on Africa's history, including the world's primordial civilizations, is vital to the healthy identity of Black young people. We hope our readers will make this a companion to *Who Dropped the Ball on Our Kids?*, which offers some strategies and suggested shifts in our collective mindset.

> *Self-understanding, racial pride, an ability to analyze the historical context and tragic experiences endured by one's people and exploring the culture and history of other non-white groups are key to developing a healthy foundation for a young person. These provide a sense of placement and continuity.* P. 149

Connections Remembered is About Memory

Memory refers to our ability to take in, retain, and when necessary, recall information and experiences contained within our brains. What we retain and recall from our past helps determine what and how we learn from and respond to daily experiences. What we remember has much to do with how we develop self-identity.

Memory has power. How and what we remember has power to shape parts or the whole of our lives. Why is it that I, Lindiwe, remember key pieces of my childhood differently than my siblings? We argue to this day about *what happened? what didn't? who was favored? who wasn't?* Each of us reports a different rendering of events. To what extent did our family upbringing affect the forming of memories that, in turn, shaped our paths, our choices, our child-rearing practices, or our ways of relating to friends and partners? What "truths" did these memories create for each of us? The good thing about our sharing what we each remember of our family history is that we have been able to construct a better, more realistic, shared memory.

For those in education, there is usually a required university course that distinguishes three types of memory—sensory, short term, and long term. At some point the classroom conversation will examine the idea of *selective* memory. The realization that even though we each have three types of memory, what sticks with each of us is selective. We don't all register, think about or store the same things. Not to mention, even when we remember the same things, we may remember them differently. It might be useful to reflect on what you tend to recall, what others recall that you don't, and importantly why. *Why do I choose to remember what I remember?* Or as our grandparents would say with sage wisdom, "You remember what you want to remember." Selective memory is apparent when earlier generations tend to remember the behaviors and events from their world, "back in the day," in more glowing terms especially when comparing them with the experiences of today's young people. They filter out or soften some aspects, while selectively choosing to amplify the best parts as if that was the whole of their existence.

The two parts of personal memory: There's direct and indirect (i.e., vicarious memory). Direct memory derives from experiences or encounters that you are a witness to or a participant in. Vicarious memory, on the other hand, is a product of stories from others and written documents. It is a personal memory acquired, even though you were not physically present. Vicarious memory adds to your connections to people, places, and events that you could not experience directly. These stories of events before you were born, often shared by parents and other older relatives, hopefully allow you to get a deeper sense of who you are.

With each of these memory types, people around us can help us piece the stories of our lives together, even those pieces we have selectively chosen to forget. This remembering becomes more urgent for us as the generations before us grow older and begin forgetting. Retrieving the stories becomes more difficult as we age. One of the most painful occurrences is witnessing a loved one's struggle with dementia, the steady loss of memory. Many of us have been through this, watching a parent's or grandparent's long bout with dementia, when they could no longer remember who their children were. Their memories often shifted back to a time 40 or 50 years before, until even those memories fade. The medical community reports that one effect of dementia is a loss of identity because of the loss of long-term memory.

This book is concerned with remembering—reconstructing our collective memory of our history. Given what has happened to Black people in Africa, the Americas and worldwide, it's not far-fetched to assume we suffer from a collective, white western system-induced dementia.

> **Given what has happened to Black people in Africa, the Americas and worldwide, it is not far-fetched to conjecture that we suffer from a collective, system-induced dementia.**

As victims of a white western process of racial memory erasure, we have nearly lost all sense of who we really are. The emergence of a destructive identity makes it nearly impossible for us to work together for our collective interests. We do not know who we really are and importantly, *all we really are* in terms of the reality and flow of historical events. We and our children are in a war to recapture our collective memory and our true and full identity.

Memory matters to identity. How much do you remember about your personal history? Imagine for instance, if something happened and you could no longer remember your name, address, parents, or your own children. The thought itself is

---

If memory is the thread of personal identity, history is the thread of community identity. – *Carl Lindberg*

---

disorienting. Who would you be? We are defined and given purpose, for better or worse, through memory. The reality today is that most Black people in America have little memory of our historical roots prior to plantation slavery. Those making the effort to find ourselves by tracing our family genealogy, most often run into dead ends because there were no laws that valued retaining our histories during chattel slavery. The painful void it leaves, the emptiness of not knowing or being cut off from *Who am I? Who are they? What happened to them?* is inexplicable. Why can't I find my lineage, while most white groups easily trace back to the European Middle Ages?

During chattel slavery, records of births, deaths, family trees, etc. were not preserved; it was deemed unnecessary, even illegal, to document details of our identity. In Rochelle Riley's wrenching book of 2018, *The Burden* (a compilation of what it is like carrying the weight of being Black), one contributor's story is called *Living Without a Beginning*. In it, Patricia Gaines says *"This 'homelessness' of the spirit ripples through decades of human living, causing unseen damage."*

Consider the indiscriminate separation of families across the South during chattel slavery, and the issues are further exacerbated. So, we are not able to go beyond a certain point as we travel backwards in time to find our family trees. This is all a part of a larger plan to keep us disconnected from any powerful racial identity, while anchoring us to a sense of self that vacillates between acting out as second-class citizens, internal rage, or perpetual self-questioning.

If we do not know our history, then we do not know our personality. And if the only history we know is other people's history then our personality has been created by that history.

Amos N. Wilson

Our short-circuited genealogy leads many to conclude we began our existence as slaves, the property of our white masters. We have been deceived into believing any life we had prior to 1619 was one of shameful barbarism and lack of culture. To 'protect us" from the shame of being connected to our African existence, all accounts of ancient Africa have been largely hidden from us. According to the white oppressors, and sadly an idea embraced by uninformed Black people, we became civilized through our contact with our slave masters and their "advanced" way of life.

Memory is influenced and manipulated to maintain the oppressor's control. One's personal memory is an extension and derivative of a common, collective memory. The information that constitutes the collective memory is a cultural phenomenon. That information is assembled and validated by those in power. In our case, that has been the white power group, who decide what information is of greatest importance to maintaining their power and wealth, while withholding any information that threatens it.

The content of our collective memory is transmitted through several cultural sources among which are: *oral tradition* (family, friends, neighbors), *the educational system* and the *web of other institutional structures*, including mass media and religious entities. The white power group ensures any messaging that runs counter to upholding white supremacy and Black inferiority is disparaged or not disclosed at all. For Black people, to maintain submission to this imposition of second-class status, we eventually became slaves within our own minds. Thus, the memory shaped by our

> **The most effective way to destroy people is to deny and obliterate their own understanding of their history.**
>
> *— George Orwell*

indoctrination in America creates what Paulo Freire calls an *"adhesion to the oppressor."* All other memories, of racial primacy, became part of our collective dementia.

Memory can be reignited with intention and effort. This is what this book helps us accomplish. ***Connections Remembered*** is one antidote to treat our collective dementia. It harkens back to our beginnings, a tapestry of monumental and productive invention spanning millions of years. We must remember.

This book is one tool to help restore our wholeness, given that everything in our Black experience in America has been designed to obliterate our historical memory. Employing the most egregious means in human history to reduce us to "less-than" status (from the transatlantic slave trade up through today's mass incarceration and subpar schools) has been critical to this aim. Replacing the scholarship of ancient

Africa with a Eurocentric, fabricated view served as a support to the dehumanization imposed upon Black people. The educational curricula since the end of chattel slavery furthered the memory erasure of ancient Africa. We need counter strategies to mitigate these psychically-damaging, institutional practices.

We can and must recapture our memory by critically studying and piecing together what we can of our African past to facilitate restoring our lost memories. We owe our young people our stories to help ground them in the powerful memory of who we were and who they are. This is part of the function of this book, ***Connections Remembered*** –to recollect and reconstruct Black memory. This is our collective ancestry.com, our 23andme.com, a critical part of our collective group genealogy.

The wider and more accurate our historical memory, the greater our sense of wholeness and rootedness, and the more powerfully affirming our identity becomes. This reclaimed identity is a necessary precursor for a unified effort to transform our condition of oppression.

Making the Best Use of This Book

The book is a guide for all those with a stake in fostering healthy racial identity among Black people, from childhood through adulthood. That might be the student of African history, the educator, the parent, the youth leader, or mentor. It is also a great resource for adults who have not had much exposure to the African foundations of humanity and civilization. This guide is designed as an easy-to-use survey and quick reference for matters related to our African antiquity.

Connections Remembered is a synthesis of the scholarship of preeminent thinkers regarding the African origins of human life, culture, and civilization. It challenges the *reasonability* of the Eurocentric model of history propagated in American schools, which fosters self-negating Black identities. We make the case for African-centered study as foundational for grounding Black young people in an affirming sense of living in their Black skins.

We hope this book is rewarding on several levels. First, it contains enough information for an abbreviated, yet well investigated study of African history, with suggestions for a more comprehensive exploration. For some, it should help when you may want to locate a few facts without searching through your library.

For those working in mentoring, Rites of Passage, and other positive identity-developing programs, we have included a few activities as you aid Black young people with uncovering the marvels of their homeland. This guide is a base from which to develop lessons, rituals, and structures for knowledge development. It won't take long for the students to begin dismantling the "backwards" notions about Africa that are so pervasive in schools and throughout U.S. culture.

Combining and condensing years of research, we bring you this concise resource guide. In it, you will find eight sections that include the following:

- Short historical narratives around key events and why they matter
- Charts that provide facts at-a-glance
- Clearly labeled maps, which can be reproduced for your use
- A listing of books to provide you deeper knowledge of each topic
- A sampling of the West African Adinkra symbols and quotable quotes from Black scholars

Sections VII and VIII were added to this edition of *Connections Remembered.* These address some questions about the bridge between the glorious African past we proudly share with readers and the 21st century reality of Black life today. *How did we end up as a despised race based solely on our skin color? What forces were put in motion for us to lose the stature of our ancient past? What factors converged to maintain Black oppression for more than 400 years?*

Notes to Educators and Study Leaders

Whether you are teaching in a school, facilitating an adult study group or a family roundtable, leading a youth Rites of Passage program or doing independent study, the issue of relevancy must be addressed for the study to have meaning and evoke deep interest. To have life-altering value, the education of African Americans, particularly children, must be consciously conceived of and pursued as a serious

The process of education within any society is never neutral, objective, or apolitical.

political and social-cultural endeavor. The process of education within any society is never neutral, objective, or apolitical. The educational system's primary function is to justify and maintain the power relationships that already exist within a society. Bertrand Russell, late British philosopher and Nobel Prize winner, illuminated this idea in 1916, saying:[1]

> *Almost all education has a political motive: it aims at strengthening some group, national or religious or even social, in the competition with other groups. It is this motive, in the main, that determines the subjects taught, the knowledge offered, and the knowledge withheld, and decides what mental habits the pupils are expected to acquire. Hardly anything is done to foster inward growth of mind and spirit; in fact, those who have had the most education are very often atrophied in their mental and spiritual health.*

This guide is written from the perspective of the fundamental political function of history and education. Those who use it should organize their lessons and conversations with the goal of developing the child's and their own capacity to perceive, analyze, and evaluate their and the Black community's existence through a political frame of reference. The lessons should prompt participants to probe deeper into the human experience by not only answering the *what happened* questions (the extent of the intellectual process in most urban public schools) but also *why and how?*

---

[1] From Education as a political institution, *The Atlantic*, June 1916

When we send our children to school, we need to be vigilant about what they are being taught and how they are processing those teachings. To navigate the Eurocentric-leaning curriculum and its presentation of history, prime our young people to explore such questions as: *Who benefitted? How have these events in history been rearranged and expressed, and to whose advantage? Why is so much of the Black historical experience excluded from the curriculum? What impact do events have on each group's self-worth and identity? What's missing in the story? What's another point of view on this same story?*

Creating and posing probing questions helps students engage and enhances higher-order thinking skills. This kind of interrogating can lead students to recognize the power dynamics at the core of every social issue and reality itself. When the oppressed begin to see their second-class status as the consequence of a historical set of unequal power relationships between and among groups, deliberately legitimized by the educational system (as part of the larger institutional network), the basis for social transformation and group self-determination will be set.

As you pursue this study, here are some considerations to guide you:

1. What is the historical narrative that is commonly accepted as true by most people, and how does it diverge from what you are reading in this book?

2. Where is this aspect of African history taught? Why and why not? What is the parallel or *other* story put in its place?

3. What value can this information have on how we behave, view ourselves, and our community?

4. How can this knowledge help us succeed individually and collectively?

5. What, if any, is my personal responsibility to help facilitate the needed change?

6. How has education impacted our collective memory?

Section 1

AFRICA

A Framework for the Study

Highlights:

1. Merits of studying African history
2. Two competing models of history

Epa (handcuffs) you are the slave of him whose handcuffs you wear

Words Worth Heeding: *Our history and our culture were completely destroyed when we were forcibly brought to America in chains. And now it is important for us to know that our history did not begin with slavery. We came from Africa, a great continent, wherein live a proud and varied people, a land which…was the cradle of civilization.* –Malcolm X

Africa's Greatness

Scientists believe the **OLDEST LIFE FORM** was found in Swaziland, in southeast Africa dating back 3.5 billion years ago.

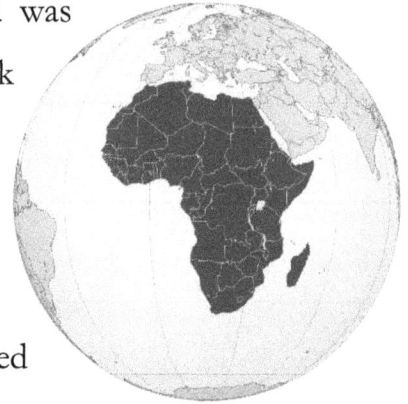

LIFE SPREAD FROM AFRICA TO THE REST OF THE WORLD. When all the continents were joined in very ancient times (called Pangaea) Africa was at the center. Africa later became the center of a southern supercontinent (Gondwanaland).

The **FIRST HUMAN ANCESTORS & THE FIRST HUMANS,** including today's "homo sapiens sapiens" **BEGAN IN AFRICA**. Humans in Africa lived 1 to 3 million years before humans did on any other continent.

The **FIRST HUMAN FAMILIES** (in Africa) are documented by archaeological and anthropological evidence to have **LIVED IN HARMONY WITH BOTH NATURE AND NEIGHBOR,** refuting the popular myth that primal humans were violent and antagonistic.

The world's **FIRST ORGANIZED SOCIETIES**, with landmark achievements, **WERE IN AFRICA, ALONG THE NILE VALLEY**. Egypt was not the oldest but is the most famed of the Nile Valley civilizations—from Uganda to the Mediterranean Sea—with art, architecture, science, medicine, religion, and universities. Culture and advanced knowledge were transported from Africa to the rest of the world.

African history is a stream and source from which we can draw power, persistence, and inspiration for our daily lives.

Check out your mind

1. Name two books about Africa's history written by Black historians.

   _____   _____

2. What are two major events in African history that you learned about when you were in school?

   _____   _____

3. What are some benefits of Black students learning African/Black history that took place *before* the slave trade?

   _____

I f African Americans prioritized studying our African past, we would witness a positive difference in the attitude and behaviors of our children and in our relationships with each other. Studying our history is about more than learning interesting facts and figures; importantly, knowledge of self is a partial remedy for racial survival and well-being. We live in a society where Black emotional health is constantly undermined by a deeply entrenched societal declaration of Black inferiority. Even in the moments when we feel fully capable and grounded, these moments can be fleeting; the assault on our very essence is always there permeating every area of our lives. The systemic racism erodes our confidence, giving way to a nagging self-questioning and self-loathing.

Accurate knowledge of one's history is as crucial as a baseball player knowing where home plate is; without this instinctive knowledge, the player is disoriented, lost in the game. Such disorientation makes it difficult for Black people to gain a foothold among the powerful nations of the world. We are constantly on the defense against physical and political assault, and without much ammunition beyond complaint and, at best, excited protestation. Until we center ourselves in a common, prideful past, we have no base from which to unite and empower ourselves. That common past, with both pride and challenge, must be recognized as one continuous flow of history beginning in Africa. **The African American historical experience is part of the same African historical journey. We have been deceived into viewing these as two separate histories. That is a part of our current predicament.** Discontinuity of history leads to discontinuity with self, and consequently a fragmenting from our past, each other, and our community.

So deficient is our race's identification with our native Motherland that our children lose the battle for healthy identity early in their formative years. This contrasts with ethnic immigrant groups who freely claim their connection to a mother or father country. They either find or construct the means to reinforce their culture, language, and solidarity. Our transport to America, dissimilar to theirs, was involuntary and psychologically and physically brutal. Reviling "blackness" and Africa were intertwined with Europeans' economic slavery enterprise, which flourished by exploiting our forebears' Black bodies. So intense was the denunciation of "blackness" that now, many generations since our "emancipation," African

Americans are still reluctant to own up to our Black African connection, often claiming "color does not matter." Some of us are so repulsed by the suggestion of a linkage to Africa, that we insist "I'm NOT African!"

Would it not be wise for American [Blacks] themselves to read a few books and do a little thinking for themselves? It is not that I would persuade [Blacks] to become communists, capitalists, or holy rollers, but whatever belief they reach, let it for God's sake be a matter of reason and not of ignorance.

W.E.B. DuBois, The World and Africa, p. 338, 1946

The face of America is transforming rapidly. It is projected to be racially browner and blacker establishing a "white minority" in the ensuing decades (projected for 2045 by policy expert William Frey).[2] This scenario is an opportunity for the advancement of Black studies which could give African Americans the capacity to assume our rightful stand in the world. We are now witnessing recently immigrated ethnic groups attempting to secure their place in the power and wealth of America. Simultaneously, we witness the heightened resistance, especially among white conservatives, to the burgeoning brown immigrant groups in America, a defensive move as whites come to grips with becoming a diminishing majority.

A number of ethnic groups, nonetheless, are unapologetically coalescing around their heritage and history as a basis to secure a stake in the power system. And among Black people, because of the enduring commitment of a cadre of culturally conscious

---

[2] Frey, William, 2018. *Diversity Explosion: How New Racial Demographics are Remaking America*, Brookings Institute Press.

African Americans, there are more parents and teachers who believe an African centered learning focus is necessary and viable as young Black people navigate their educational process. Our children must re-center themselves in *our* history.

> *To a very great extent the problem with the education of Black children, the crack epidemic and all of these other things we complain about day in and day out, are the results of a psychology that flows from a particular type of historical experience.* [3] P. 21

Black children are educated in a school environment where much energy is expended on name-calling, with some favored epithets like "ugly", "big lips", "nigga" and "black" (meant as derogatory) along with a slew of profanities. These young people have no idea of the direct connection between the belittling of African history and their current bleak American experience. They do not grasp that their self-concepts are marred by their conditioned, handed-down negative view of their racial past. In African-centered schools, it is a pivotal moment when the young men and women begin calling each other "brother" or "sister" rather than "nigga." This self-negation is a product of entrenched white supremacy, against which we must keep fighting. Damon Young expressed this powerfully in his 2019 book, *What Doesn't Kill You Makes You Blacker.*

> *White supremacy is so gargantuan and mundane that sometimes its existence and its proficiency can't be measured, addressed, or even seen without a stark change in perspective.* **It isn't _like_ gravity. It _is_ gravity.** *It is a ceaseless pressure intended to keep blackness ground-bound and sick.* P. 81

---

[3] Amos Wilson. 1993. *Falsification of Afrikan consciousness.* African World Infosystems.

The struggle to resurrect and maintain a healthy self and group consciousness must be unwavering. Neither we nor our children can afford to view Black history and culture as a fad relegated to the month of February. The issues of race, history, identity, and culture are ones that greatly determine who runs the world, even who runs our neighborhoods.

During the early 20th century, Dr. W.E.B. DuBois advocated for Black and African studies. This, he believed, was a requisite piece of Black folks' real emancipation and enfranchisement. Racial uplift required that moment when a critical mass of Black people from *"puzzled contemplation of a half-known self, rises to the powerful assertion of a self, conscious of its might.*[4]*"*

Cultural study holds keys to such daily enigmatic questions as: *Where can we turn for strength in a world that still views Black skin as despicable—a mistake of creation? From what reserve are we to garner the energy to keep swimming against the tide of anti-Black politics and economics? How can we reach the fullness of our potential when we have been taught and conditioned to second-guess our every action?* Historical study is one source from which we can draw strength, persistence, and power; it can help us nourish tattered roots and bind broken bridges.

Merits of Studying History

We have already noted the power of history and memory to influence and shape a people's lives. Here we want to provide specific value statements regarding exposing our young people and ourselves to the transformative potential of building our lives

---

[4] Dubois, W. E. B. 2001. *The Education of black people: Ten critiques, 1906-1960,* Herbert Aptheker, editor, new edition, Monthly Review Press

on the foundation of our history. **Historical knowledge nurtures leadership**. Black people need leaders—at every level, in every field and in every generation. We

We need all minds turned on! Effective Black leadership requires cultural and historical fluency.

are accustomed to having one or two people considered *our* leaders. Yet as schools, communities, and families, we should stimulate the leadership potential of all our young people. **We need all minds turned on!** Effective Black leadership requires cultural and historical fluency. Many of our celebrated leaders, each with a solid grounding in our history, died prematurely assassinated, brokenhearted, betrayed, confused. They often felt alone—acting as singular charismatic, sacrificial lambs, heroic leaders. Malcolm X perished at 40, Marcus Garvey at 53, Dr. King at 38, Medgar Evers at 37, Fred Hampton at 21, South Africa's Steven Biko at 30, and Kwame Touré at 57. Each, steeped in the truth of our African genius, left a leadership void which either took years to fill or has yet to be filled. That is why we need a full pipeline of leaders in every generation. Students must be taught our history and culture alongside other subjects. This means studying our rich African past, along with the genocidal and survival stories of our tragic *Maafa* (suffering). Through the glory and the agony of our past, weakness and fear must be weaned so that legions of courageous and committed young leaders can emerge.

African history grounds, reinforces and fortifies our children. Taught correctly, our history shouts, "Yes, we can," no matter how difficult things appear. It helps make our children into neighbors, friends, sisters, and brothers. It gives them grounds for perceiving and understanding the root causes for the miserable environment so common to their schools and communities, and not accept it as the norm. It helps them channel their outrage and transform cynicism into productive activity. History grounds and connects Black children to self and community, giving them an anchor for a secure and positive sense of racial identity and self-worth as they mature into adolescence and adulthood. There are many alumni from Detroit's African-centered schools that attest to the lifelong value of cultural study. In public school academies such as Detroit's Marcus Garvey, Nsoroma, Malcolm X, Mae Jemison, Aisha Shule and Paul Roberson, the centrality of African history was essential in developing kinships between young people, rather than antagonism.

In a March 2019 article on a Detroit news site, *Chalkbeat*, one teacher remarked that after teaching in both traditional classrooms and African-centered classrooms, she preferred the latter. She saw first-hand the connections being built between the students and teachers. Students refer to teachers as Mama and Baba ("mother", "father" in Swahili). Imagine, too, the multiplier effect of coupling African-centered education with the already established benefits of Black students having Black teachers. One study states: [5]

> *Black students who have just one black teacher in elementary school are more likely to graduate and more likely to enroll in college – and significantly more likely if they have two black teachers.*

African history is a framework to understand every other academic discipline. The history of Africa is the starting point for all other histories; this is well-documented. We make sense of the historical social forces that define the relationships between groups based on this grounding in our history. All curricular

---

[5] Camera, Lauren. Black teachers improve outcomes for black students, *U.S. News and World Report*, November 23, 2018

themes including history, psychology, language arts, social and legal policy, the arts, and sciences are most useful to Black students (really, *all* students) when grounded in an African-centered perspective. **Since all education is viewed and influenced by *someone's* worldview, our children must advocate for examining the interactions of groups through their historical perspective.**

Students must learn to analyze their textbooks to escape intellectual captivity. Every school curriculum (and every teacher) has an implicit cultural-historical worldview from which their work and thinking derive. This perspective determines what knowledge and interpretations are deemed "legitimate." Each student is *trained* to view themselves and the world through that cultural prism. What is real and of the highest value for the child is determined by the cultural-historical foundation upon which the curriculum is developed. Therefore, children must be encouraged to be wary and inquisitive enough to discover what perspective is being promoted. Is it being taught from an historically, accurate African center or from a Eurocentric center? Even when matriculating a subject as seemingly innocuous as art, for example, students must interrogate the curriculum, contemplating and challenging: *Whose art is being venerated? What culture is represented? What culture is not represented?*

Another recent example of the persistent creation of historical narratives intent on skewing the readers' perspective toward Black inferiority appeared recently in a <u>New York Times</u> story (1/12/2020). Titled *Two States. Eight Textbooks. Two American Stories*, columnist Dana Goldstein shows, in just one example among many, how the Black Harlem Renaissance is presented. In a California textbook, this period of great Black literature is noted as having a lasting impact, while the Texas textbook says critics questioned the *quality* of the literature. Same subject, different messaging.

History is more important than you might think!

> Whoever controls history, especially its interpretation, controls the minds and actions of the recipients of that history.

History provides a point of origin and an anchor for a group. *Where did we start? Did we start on a slave ship, or did we have our own self-governing land? Do I have kinspeople in other places?*

It clarifies the on-going historical relationship between one group and other groups. *Were we ever on top? How long? How did we get into our present political-economic situation? How long have we been oppressed and why? Is it due to a curse or human activity?*

It links past, present and future; whatever we do will set the foundation for the kind of future our children and their children have. *What kind of future do we want for ourselves and the world? What will we each do to help actualize these goals?*

It helps a group understand and respect its unique culture and rituals. *Are you ashamed or pride-filled about African symbols? Do you try to learn about them?*

It provides incentive for a group to struggle to preserve or regain dignity and self-sufficiency in a global society of competing groups. *Does our group have stature among the nations of the world? Do we have the will to commit to the collective uplift of our group?*

History provides a people with a continuum that links the present with the past and future. The student of history grasps that African history and African American history form a single, unbroken narrative. Historian John Henrik Clarke viewed history as "a current event," our home base for living today. Without a solid, continuous flow, a historical mooring, people exist in a psychological time warp. They teeter back and forth and find it difficult to answer the existential questions of *Who am I? Who are we?* The sense that life is a collection of disparate parts is not unusual for those without an identifiable and healthy placement in the human continuum of past, present, and future. The belief that Black people's beginnings were on a slave ship is the WORST kind of story to tell our children. **Even if we cannot trace our family genealogies back to our origins, tell the children why we can't!** Our history was deliberately erased to ensure we lose ourselves in service to a slave system designed to build white wealth. History connects our yesterdays and points a direction for the future.

> **Without a solid, continuous flow, a historical mooring, people exist in a psychological time warp—lost in space and time.**

> *One must be anchored in one's self, people, history, i.e., culture, before one can truly be a whole participant in a world culture or multi-culturalism; we must always start local in order to appreciate and incorporate the positive agents of the universal.[6]* P. 10

---

[6] Madhubuti, H.R. and Madhubuti, S.L. 1991. *African centered education: It's value, importance, and necessity in the development of Black children.*

History gives meaning to our search for truth. A student of history must recognize they are in a search for truth. This means evaluating not only objective facts and events, but also contemplating the subjective experiences of the author and the people about whom the story is being told. The astute pupil of history ensures that the relevance of the facts, within the context of a *specific* group's experience, is not obscured. For example, how history contextualizes the role and activism of the Black Panther Party depends on whether it is viewed through the lens of the white power establishment or through the Black communities' eyes, among whom they sought to encourage self-reliance. The first view would make it reasonable, "a matter of public safety" for the FBI to infiltrate and destroy the organization using propaganda that incited a fear of violence against the government. From the other perspective, children and families uplifted by and benefiting from the feeding initiatives, establishment of Black owned businesses, messages of self-love, legally armed community policing, etc. hailed them not as a threat but as champions for the race. With white people controlling the historical accounting, the messaging and institutional system ultimately won this unequal contest for control of the message and how people thought about the Black Panther Party. The Party was ultimately infiltrated, decimated, and left as a shadow of what it once was.

An opinion piece by Chastity Pratt on February 19, 2019, titled *The miseducation of Michigan: How state fails kids in Black history* (bridgemi.com), reiterates the deliberate misrepresentation or omission of the positive aspects of Black history and dismisses the hallmark achievements prior to the European enslavement of Blacks in Africa. The author noted that a suburban Detroit school (with a majority white student population) distributed a syllabus to the students in their African American History course. Under the section, Civil Rights Until Today, there was to be coverage of "The Boyz N the Hood" and "Inside the Crips and the Bloods," movies glorifying Black gang violence. What was the intention here, given the range of events they could have addressed over this 60 to 70-year period? Fortunately, the author's son, in search of truth, found this incredulous and insulting, then informed his mother. They put a halt to this mockery of Black history, forcing the faculty to rethink the topic.[7]

History, more than an objective report, is the unfolding of the story that lies within each event interpreted through the eyes of the "historian." History is a part of molding the range of behaviors, thought patterns, and beliefs students adopt that could impact them throughout their lives. This need for recognizing the self and group defining nature of history is noted by John H. Clarke:

> *History is a clock that people use to tell their political and cultural time of day. It is also a compass that people use to find themselves on the map of human geography. The role of history is to tell a people what they have been and where they have been, what they are and where they are. The most important role that history plays is that it has the function of telling a people where they still must go and what they still must be.*[8] P. 29

Two Competing Models of History

If all these astonishing things took place in Africa, as Afrocentrists and others assert, it could make you wonder, why isn't African history a fundamental part of public education? It seems paradoxical that so much of the world's development is owed to

---

[7] Dawsey, C. P. Opinion: the miseducation of Michigan: How state fails kids in black history. *Bridgemi.com*, 2/19/19
[8] quoted in A. Browder. 1994. *Nile Valley contributions to civilization.*

Africa; yet getting access to this knowledge is usually seen as extracurricular. There's February's Black History Month, which typically offers up a carefully curated list of simple biographies of "acceptable" Black individuals. Such lists almost always exclude events that pre-date Black plantation slavery. To know ourselves fully, we need serious conversation about seizing control of both the content and *interpretation* of historical events.

History is not unbiased, **objective reality**. An examination of each history textbook informs the reader regarding *who* is doing the story telling and what that historian's worldview is. The observant student is wary and channels this skepticism into taking the "historical facts" and exploring alternative perspectives through which to view those facts. Black students especially need to understand there are two competing viewpoints through which history is taught to them.

Martin Bernal's *Black Athena[9] Volumes I and II* have contributed to our understanding of how history is interpreted, particularly African history. He describes two approaches to the study and interpretation of history. In his discussion,

The ancient (African) model of history had primacy until the rise of modern Europe around the middle of the 18th Century.

he disavows the notion that history is purely objective. Instead, he presents the reader with two competing models of history: an ancient (African) model and the modern Eurocentric one. His work is significant in its role in the deconstruction of the

---

[99] Bernal, M. 1987. *Black Athena.*

Eurocentric view of world history. The ancient model of history had primacy until the rise of modern Europe around the middle of the 18th Century.

The European-centered view now dominates the thinking of Americans and other groups abroad. One example that demonstrates how this Eurocentric perspective maintains a stronghold is through the seemingly benign gesture of shipping American history and other textbooks to post-apartheid South African children. Americans are lauded for this goodwill, and there is little outcry among Black people over this practice of indoctrinating Black South African children to white supremacy through its white images and white-washed view of human history. During a recent visit to Ghana, our travel group was encouraged, even prodded to bring Black dolls and books with positive images of Black people. Why? Because of the scarcity of such images, unbelievably, in AFRICA. The good news is that the beautiful Ghanaian children were ecstatic to receive the books! We have a long way to go because we are still being *bamboozled* by white supremacist tactics in the 21st Century.

The Impact of this Concocted Eurocentric Model of History. The Eurocentric model, also referred to as the Aryan model, has only recently (within the context of historical time) taken precedence over the ancient model of history. For the last 200 years or so, this view was promulgated throughout the western educational system especially after elementary education became legally mandatory beginning with Massachusetts in 1852.

Why did the European historians have a need, after hundreds of years of academic validation and acceptance, to change the universally accepted model of history? Until mandatory education was enacted in the U.S., it would not have mattered much. The sociologist Ana Marie Villegas[10] maintains that education is always a political enterprise: "*School is a political institution that contributes to the perpetuation of the existing class structure.*" The lens through which people are educated has an influence on the maintenance or eventual alteration in how power and wealth are distributed in a society. So, the creation of a new orthodoxy in viewing history during the 19th Century must be viewed within the larger context of power and culture.

"School is a political institution that contributes to the perpetuation of the existing class structure."

The Eurocentric model posits that Europe (by way of Greece) was the origin and foundation of civilization. This model denies ancient Africa its advanced civilization. So, it is not by happenstance that during the last few hundred years, Africa has been depicted as a primitive, backward place populated by heathens in need of a civilizing influence. In this Euro-centric view, whites came to our rescue, and Black people became known as the "White Man's Burden."

Bernal, in his first volume, advocated for relinquishing the lies and returning to the accurate ancient model. Though he warns this will not be an easy undertaking:

If I am right in urging the overthrow of the Aryan model and its replacement by the revised ancient model, it will be necessary not only to rethink the fundamental bases of western civilization but also to recognize the penetration of racism and continental chauvinism into all our historiography or philosophy of writing history. P. 2

---

[10] Villegas. A. p. 260

Ongoing exposure to the Aryan model of history has resulted in most people of African descent, both on the African continent and in the Diaspora, viewing themselves and the world through the frame of Eurocentric cultural white supremacist ideas. The oppression, impoverishment, and dependency upon a racist system to survive, experienced in some way by all people of African descent, are bolstered by this Aryan model of history. This model reinforces a pathological psychology in both Black and white people, grounded in the myth of white supremacy and Black inferiority. This mindset makes both groups co-conspirators in the maintenance of a global system of white power and Black powerlessness. Restoring the science-based ancient African model of history as the basis for educating Black young people (actually, all children), is a central element in the effort to balance the racial power dynamic. This begins with reclaiming a racially healthy self-identification among Black people.

The Eurocentric model of history took shape over time, beginning as early as the 15th and 16th centuries alongside the "Age of European Exploration," through the rise of colonialism and the brutal enslavement of African people. This model, with it the concept of the "White Man's Burden" served to justify the inhumane rape of the African continent and the wanton abuses surrounding the *Maafa* (Suffering). During that period, European anthropologists and clergy **created a view** of African people organized around an all-encompassing declaration of Black inferiority, a deeply held idea from which most are not yet completely free today. Books and papers were published by esteemed European professors purporting to *prove* the innate inferiority of Black people.

Two Competing Models of History

Did you know that the common view of the history of the world held today only became popular over the last approximately 250 years? It is a REVISED view, which contradicts scientific evidence. Which view do you accept?

	Eurocentric (Revised)	Afrocentric (Ancient)
Time dimension	Recent	Ancient
Location of origin	Western world	Eastern world
General ethos	I-centered	We-centered
Behavior	Competition, self-interest, individualism	Cooperation, group interest, communalism
Social outcomes	Alienation, distrust, loneliness	Belonging, interdependence
Religion	Ideas/dogma	Experiential/spiritualism

This western historical paradigm is premised on blatant distortions and omissions of historical events. It is also the basis of a view of history that dominates American school systems and conditions a feeling of inferiority among Black children because of the color of their skins and superiority for whites because of theirs. The effort to give veracity to the Eurocentric model and its declaration of Black inferiority has been so pervasive and consistent that it is embedded in the psyche of both Black and white people.

In contrast, the ancient **African model of history** dominated the world for thousands of years, since the dawn of recorded history. It is based on the evidence of historians prior to the rise of Europe and indicates the major portion of the ancient civilized world was a Black African one. Says J. A. Rogers:

> *With the rise of white racism, whose real aim was to justify the enslavement of blacks, certain noted scholars denied that the Egyptians were black. They were pure white, they assert. But Herodotus saw them. They did not.*[11] P.11

As the "father of history," Herodotus was eyewitness to their blackness.

Based on the ancient model, Greece, the foundation of white western civilization, attained much of its knowledge and culture from a long-term relationship with African people. Africa is the mother of civilization, and all others are her offspring.

The ancient model provides an approach to world history which correctly situates Africa as the center and point of origin for life and civilization, not Greece. The findings of esteemed African, Asian, and European scientists and scholars support

---

[11] Rogers, J.A. 1989. *Africa's gift to America.*

this view (e.g., Herodotus, Homer, Godfrey Higgins, Louis Leakey, John Jackson, Chancellor Williams, Cheikh Anta Diop, and Basil Davidson). Africa lent the gifts of civilization to the world.

To undermine the ancient African model of history, erroneous descriptions and labels for peoples and places in Africa were employed in order to de-Africanize them: e.g., Berbers, Hamites, Semites, Pygmies, brown and red peoples. Be cautious when you come across these labels as you study Africa's history. Egypt, with its record of superlative achievement in ancient times, is still being dealt with as though it is not an African land. One of the 20th Century ploys is the establishment of a region called the "Middle East"—another tactic to discredit or de-Africanize Black achievement.

The next section takes a closer look at our Motherland Africa, the land, its geography, and its natural features.

Section 1: IN ACTION

How much do you know about your placement in history?

1. On the lines below, list 5 or more historical events (or people) in the Black American experience that took place before your birth.

   _____   _____
   _____   _____
   _____   _____
   _____   _____
   _____   _____

2. Now list 5 or more events or significant people in our African history BEFORE Black people were brought to America in human bondage.

   _____   _____
   _____   _____
   _____   _____
   _____   _____
   _____   _____

3. Compare your lists with others and share what you have in common and why you chose those events.

4. Identify two Black history authors whose writings help elevate the achievements of Black people.

   _____   _____

These events and people helped shaped who you are,

whether you realize it or not.

Know thyself and you shall be free.

Section 2

AFRICA

A Magnificent Land & its Geography

Highlights:

1. The location and physical size of Africa
2. The geography of Africa
3. Africa's countries and timeline of independence

Mframadan (wind house); house built to stand windy and treacherous conditions

Words Worth Heeding: *We seek to no longer be victimized by others as to our place in the center of world history. We do this not because of arrogance but because it is necessary to place Africa at the center of our existential reality, else we will remain detached, isolated and spiritually lonely people.* –Molefi K. Asante

Africa's dimensions in relation to the other of the earth's land masses are significant because dimensionality, comparison and proportion are emphasized in America, and affect attitudes.

Check out your mind

1. Taking the definition of a continent as "a land mass surrounded *on all sides* by water," how many continents are there? _____

    List them. _____

    _____

2. Name any three bodies of water in Africa.

    _____ _____ _____

3. When did African nations begin declaring their independence from white colonial rule? Which was the first nation to do so?

    _____ _____

Africa, the land. The study of the African continent, as a physical entity, is astonishing. It includes many of the world's firsts, some of the longest and the biggest in terms of natural phenomena. Unfortunately, many African American students have, along with other American students, a general aversion to geography, thus have limited competence related to Africa's location and importance. Africa's dimensions, especially in relation to the other of the earth's lands, matter because dimensionality, scale, and proportion are emphasized in America. They influence attitudes and viewpoints. These variables are often manipulated to meet the aims of those in power. Eurocentric historians have devoted considerable effort to comparing physical sizes and attributes that diminish anything about Africa and African people—brain size, height, color, etc. Maps used by the white nations of Europe and North America are known for exaggerating these lands' size and reducing the size of nations of color—Africa, Asia, and South America. Newer world maps that attempt to present the "actual" size of the land masses are based on what is called **Peters Projection**. Physically, Africa surpasses most of the world's land masses in size and in regard to contributions to the origins of humanity and civilization.

Africa is a CONTINENT

- **Africa is nearly 12 million square miles.**
- **Including Madagascar, Africa is three times the size of Europe, a third larger than the entire North American continent, and four times the size of the United States (a country so it should not be compared at all, but often is).**
- **Africa is 5,000 miles long and 4, 600 miles wide.**
- **Africa makes up 20.4% of the earth's land.**

Africa is very big!

Some facts about Africa's natural features

The Continents of the World

Continents	Square miles
Asia	16,990,000
AFRICA	11,700,000
North America	8,500,000
South America	6,800,000
Antarctica	5,000,000
Europe*	3,800,000
Australia	2,900,000

formerly recognized as a western extension of Asia

Africa's Major Rivers

Name	Location	Length (miles)	Empties into
Nile	Central & NE	4,100	Mediterranean Sea
Congo	Central	2,900	Atlantic Ocean
Niger	West	2,590	Gulf of Guinea
Zambezi	Southeast	1,650	Indian Ocean

Africa's Popular Archaeological Sites

Present Country	Sites
Kenya & Tanzania	(Great Lakes region) Olduvai Gorge and Laetoli, Tanzania; Lake Turkana, Kenya
Ethiopia	Omo and Hadar
South Africa	Klasies River Mouth and Border Cave

The Location and Enormity of Africa

To reiterate, Africa is a CONTINENT, not a country. It is a continent whose make up includes many countries. The United States should not be compared to Africa, because the United States is a COUNTRY, a part of the North American continent, which includes 23 countries (including many Caribbean islands, Canada, and the United States). Africa has more *countries* than the United States has states. This is often obscured because American media and historians have a habit of juxtaposing the continent of Africa with the United States, a country. This is not a harmless comparison. It is part of the Eurocentric view cast over all the institutional systems, including schools. News journalists graphically represent Africa and the contiguous United States (excluding Hawaii and Alaska) as though they are roughly the same size, which is absurd. The contiguous United States is approximately three million square miles and can be placed inside of Africa about four times (see diagram to the left); Africa measures 11.7 million square miles and is the second largest CONTINENT, exceeded in size only by Asia. One sign of basic cultural and historical fluency we hope to achieve would be when Black folks encounter our African-born brethren and upon hearing that

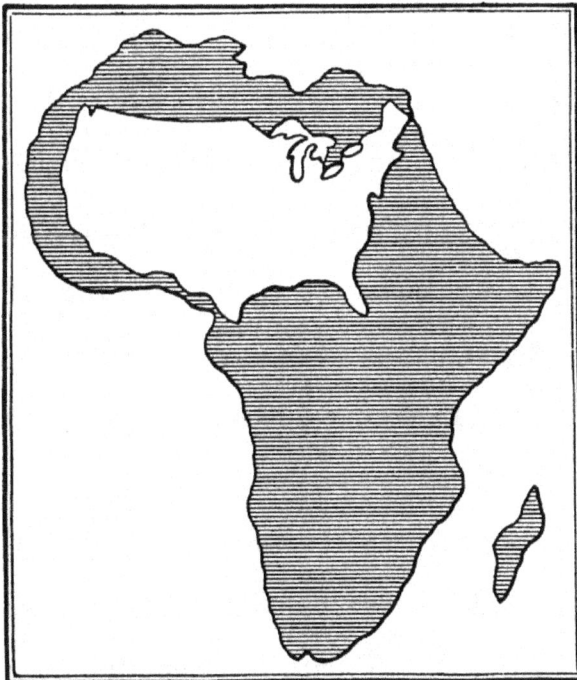

beautiful accent, we ask: Where are you from? And he or she says Africa, we can follow up with, *What part? Which country?* After their initial shock that you realized Africa is not a monolithic country, you can visualize where the country is located.

One sign of basic historical fluency is when Black folks encounter our African-born brethren. Then upon hearing that beautiful accent, we ask: *Where are you from?* And they say Africa, we ask, *Which country?* After their shock that you realized Africa is not a monolithic country, you conjure a visual image of where the country is located. Then we can engage in better conversations about our common home. That's small, but a beginning.

Then we can ask even better questions and engage in conversation about our shared connection and common home. That's small, but a beginning.

Despite the enormity of Africa and the fact that much of our livelihood is tied to the world's land masses, students should also know **nearly three-quarters of the earth's surface is water.** The land upon which humanity dwells is surrounded by massive amounts of water. Living in crowded, urban areas tends to isolate many African Americans from water, such that a good number develop abnormal fears about it. Some have conjectured that this phobia may be related to the deep trauma associated with our brutal transport from western Africa to the Americas, where the Atlantic Ocean became a vast cemetery for Black bodies belonging to those who were either thrown overboard or valiantly jumped overboard to escape the misery and stench of the slave vessels. Nonetheless, Black people had hundreds even thousands of years of prolific achievements associated with water, including the spread of original humanity and culture along Africa's waterways.

The earth's waterways, as of the 2000s, include five major oceans. These are, in order of size:

1. **Pacific Ocean** (64+ million square miles). It is large enough for the entire world's land surface to fit into it and still have room left over.
2. **Atlantic Ocean** (33.4 million square miles.) It is approximately half the size of the Pacific Ocean.
3. **Indian Ocean** (28.4 million square miles).
4. **Southern Ocean** (20.3 million square miles). It was recently classified as an ocean (in 2000) and is also known as the **Antarctic Ocean**.
5. **Arctic Ocean** (5.1 million square miles).

71% of the Earth's Surface is Water

Africa is one of seven continents. If we were to be literal, by definition, there are six continents, not seven. These make up the other 25-30% of the earth's surface. Interestingly, Europe is considered a continent, even though it does not fit the classic definition, which commonly considered a continent to be one of the earth's large continuous land masses surrounded *on all sides* by water. One American geographer, J.E. Fairchild noted in 1964:

> *Europe is thought of as a separate continent. However, Europe is a westward extension of Asia; it is part of the same land mass.*

Since Asia and Europe constitute one continuous land mass, in previous centuries, this mass was commonly referred to as Eurasia. Most dictionaries today no longer use that definition—allowing for the one exception, Europe. Again, Eurocentric authors manipulated history to elevate Europe by declaring it a separate continent.

The Geography of Africa

Africa is in the world's **eastern hemisphere** (one of the earth's halves, divided in two by a meridian), along with Eurasia (Europe and Asia), Australia and Antarctica. Africa is 5,000 miles long (from North to South) and 4,000 miles wide. Africa is joined to Eurasia at the Straits of Gibraltar (at the northwest corner) and at the Isthmus of Suez (in the northeast). Fitting the traditional definition of continent, Africa is bounded by waterways on all sides, which include:

- The Mediterranean Sea on the north
- The Red Sea and Gulf of Aden on the east
- The Indian Ocean on the east and south
- The Atlantic Ocean on the west and south

Africa's Waterways, Mountains, and Deserts

The world's longest river is in Africa. The Nile, in northeastern Africa, begins at two points: The White Nile at Lake Victoria (in Uganda) in central Africa and the Blue Nile at Lake Tana (in Ethiopia). These two converge and the Nile then **flows northward**, empties into the Mediterranean Sea, and is 4,100 miles long. In a weak, but often-made comparison, the longest river in North America is the Missouri River, which is 2,466 miles long. Not only is the Nile the longest river in the world, humanity was birthed along its tributaries in central east Africa. The ancient Nile Valley history is a voluminous record of achievement. It is no wonder that every effort is made to take Egypt, thus the Nile, out of Africa, by Eurocentrists.

Waterways are significant because they are known to contribute to the peopling of a land, providing water for farming and transportation. In addition to the Nile, Africa has many other major and historically significant rivers. These include the Niger,

Congo, Zambezi, Orange, Senegal, and Gambia. Great cultures were established and thrived along these rivers.

Africa is also home to some significant lakes. While we are familiar with America's Great Lakes, Africa has its own (and older) system of great lakes with an ancient history which earns the designation of "great." The African great lakes (see map to the right) are in central east Africa's Rift Valley. The most notable of the ten are Lakes Victoria, Tanganyika, Malawi, Turkana, Edward, Kivu, and Albert. Lake Victoria is second in size, following the U.S.'s Lake Superior, as the world's largest freshwater lakes. This region has for centuries been a hot spot for excavation teams seeking the remains of the first humans and the world's first cultures. It was in this area that the remains of the earliest humans were found. Lake Chad is another of Africa's well-known lakes and is in the country by that name in central Africa.

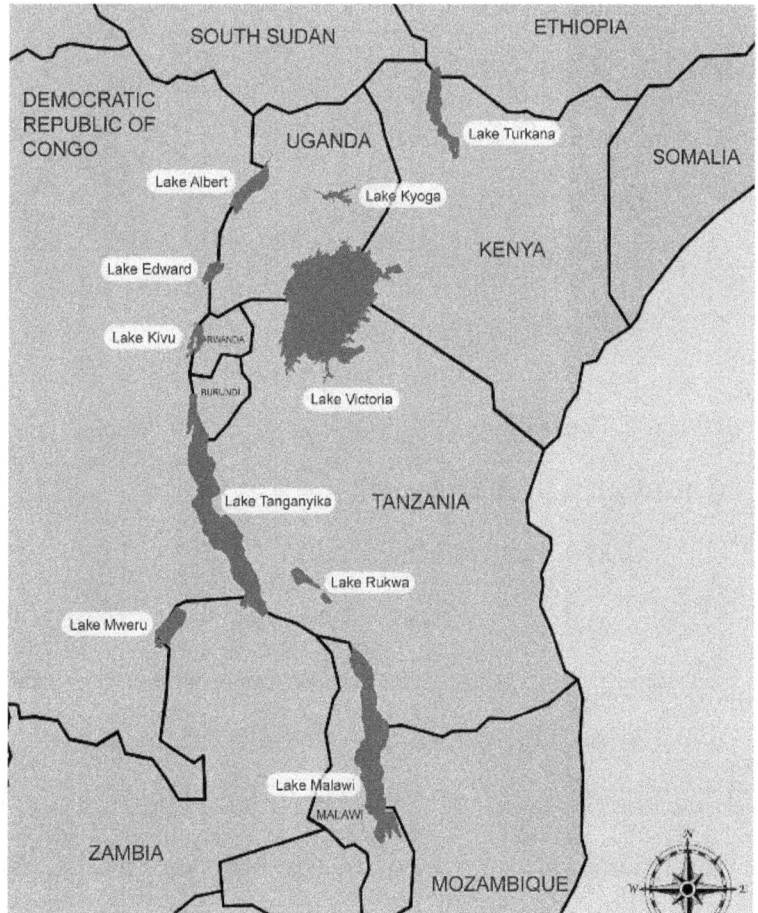

Africa's Topography. Though we mostly hear about either Africa's tropical rainforests or its arid conditions (which contribute to much of Africa's famine and hunger), Africa is a land of diverse topography. **Africa's major land types are rain forests, mountains, savannas, and deserts.** Equatorial Africa is known for its heavy rainfalls, dense forests, swamps, and streams. This area makes up much of the equatorial rain forest, the home of many exotic animals, such as crocodiles, snakes, monkeys, and gorillas. Eighteen percent of the world's rainforests are in this region. The savannas, which lie just above and below the equator, are tropical grasslands.

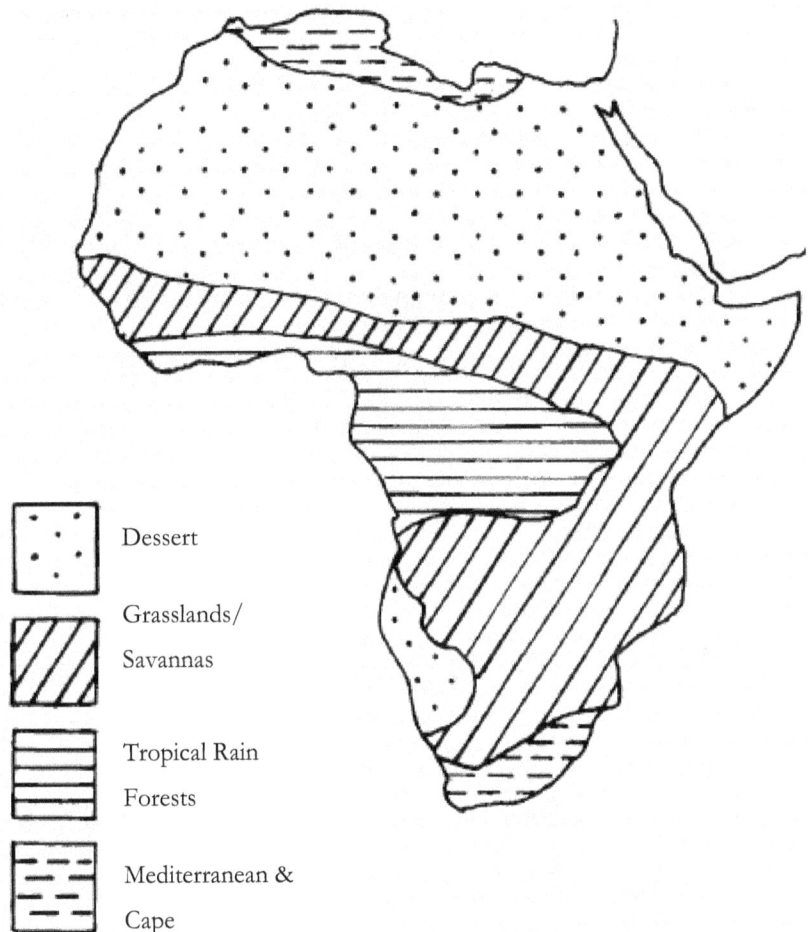

Dessert

Grasslands/
Savannas

Tropical Rain
Forests

Mediterranean &
Cape

With a short rainy season, the grass grows rapidly and is often dry. This makes for good animal grazing; thus, certain animals that feed on grass live in abundance there—giraffes, rhinoceros, antelopes, and zebras.

Then, there are the deserts. The two great deserts of Africa are the **Sahara** (the largest in the world) and the **Kalahari** (of southern west Africa). Though the Sahara Desert forms an almost impenetrable barrier between the northern coastal African countries and the lands of central and southern Africa, in former times (as late as 3000 b.c.) Africans traveled freely without obstruction because the area was not a vast, formidable desert. The Sahara Desert began expanding thousands of years ago and is expected to continue.

The earliest culture of Europe (in Greece) emerged as a result of civilized Africans migrating to the Mediterranean island of Crete before the Sahara region dried up about 3,000 b.c. This idea of a unified Africa—north and south, is important to our understanding and deconstruction of the myth of a Black (sub-Saharan) and a non-Black Africa (northern coastal).

Africa has several noteworthy mountains. The major ones are:

- Ruwenzori Range (central east Africa)
- Atlas Mountains (northwestern Africa)
- Mount Kilimanjaro (the highest peak in Africa; located in Tanzania)
- Mount Kenya (Kenya)
- Drakensberg Mountains (southern Africa)

Of these, Africa's **Ruwenzori Range** is a renowned focal point for archaeologists' fossil searches to fathom human origins, study early human migratory patterns, and investigate the shifting earth's tectonic plates (See Section 3).

Regarding natural resources, Africa is believed to be **the richest continent in the world.** Not only has Africa been a tremendous reservoir for the European (and others') exploitation of humans and culture, it is still highly sought after for the valuables beneath its earth. These riches play a key role in the unrelenting assault on Africa. The mineral riches include diamonds, gold, bauxite, manganese, nickel, platinum, cobalt, lithium, copper, uranium ore, oil, and rubber.

One modern source put it this way: Africa hides 40% of the potential hydroelectric supply, 90% of the world's cobalt, 50% of the phosphates, 40% of the platinum, 7.5% of the coal, 8% of the known petroleum reserves, 12% of natural gas and 3% of the iron ore. Africa has 60% of the world's most fertile farmland. Africa also is the source of much of the world's diamond and chromium wealth. *"Arguably, no other continent is blessed with so much in abundance and diversity."*[12]

Sampling of Africa's Wealth of Natural Resources

Bauxite	Gold	Oil/petroleum
Chromium	Iron	Phosphates
Coal	Lithium	Platinum
Copper	Manganese	Rubber
Diamonds	Nickel	Uranium

[12] Lamb, David. 1983. *Africans*. Random House, p. 20

The Countries of Africa Today

There are **54 countries on the African continent, more than on any of the seven other "recognized" continents**. (*estimates*: "Europe" has 46 countries, Asia 48, North America 23, South America 12, Antarctica 0, and Australia 3). Much of the tribal group conflict and division between African countries are the tragic culmination of the **European Partition of Africa of 1884-1885**. This ruthless "divide and conquer" power grab established new tribal and national boundaries. They divvied up these newly carved nations among the various white European imperialists. Subsequently, efforts to maintain the indigenous national lines led to inter-tribal wars. Though Africa continues to address the impact of these imposed polarizing lines of separation, as evidenced by brutal territorial struggles and civil wars between nations and peoples (e.g. 1975-2002 Angola's MPLA and UNITA and 1990-1994 Hutus and Tutsis), all the countries are, at least, free of *formal* colonial rule. The last to gain independence was South Africa when Nelson Mandela was elected president in 1994.

The map and present list of 54 African countries are on the following pages. The most recently established independent country is South Sudan, which broke from Sudan in 2011.

Hopefully, the establishment of Africa's geographic location, dimensions, and diverse tapestry offer enough foundational information to engage our African-born brothers and sisters in more meaningful dialogue. Explore the map and lists; then we will move to Africa's placement in the historical origins of humanity and culture.

Africa: a continent with MANY COUNTRIES

Africa's countries, capitals, year of independence

Country	Capital	Population (millions, estimates)	Location (general)	Year Independent	Prior Colonizer
1. *Algeria*	Algiers	43.0	NE	7.3.1962	France
2. *Angola*	Luanda	31.8	SW	11.11.1975	Portugal
3. *Benin*	Porto-Novo	11.8	W	8.1.1960	France
4. *Botswana*	Gaborone	2.3	S	9.30.1966	Britain
5. *Burkina Faso (formerly Upper Volta)*	Ouagadougou	20.3	W	8.1.1960	France
6. *Burundi*	Gitega (2019)	11.5	E-Central	7.1.1962	Belgium
7. *Cameroon*	Yaoundé	25.9	West	1.1.1960	France
8. *Cape (Cabo) Verde*	Praia	.5	W-Island	7.5.1975	Portugal
9. *Central African Republic*	Bangui	4.7	Central	8.13.1960	France
10. *Chad*	N'Djamena	15.9	Central	8.11.1960	France
11. *Comoros*	Moroni	.9	E-Island	7.6.1975	France
12. *Congo*	Brazzaville	5.4	W-Central	8.15.1960	France
13. *Cote d'Ivoire*	Yamoussoukro & Abidjan	25.8	W	8.7.1960	France
14. *Democratic Rep. of Congo (formerly Zaire)*	Kinshasa	86.7	Central	6.30.1960	Belgium
15. *Djibouti*	Djibouti	.98	NE	7.27.1977	France
16. *Egypt (Kemet)*	Cairo	100.3	NE	2.28.1922	Britain
17. *Equatorial Guinea*	Malabo	1.4	W	10.12.1968	Spain
18. *Eswatini (Swaziland)*	Mbabane/ Lobamba	1.1	SE	9.6.1968	Britain
19. *Ethiopia*	Addis Ababa	112.0	East	5.5.1941	Italy
20. *Eritrea*	Asmara	3.5	East	5.24.1993	Ethiopia
21. *Gabon*	Libreville	2.2	West	8.16.1960	France
22. *Gambia*	Banjul	2.3	West	2.18.1965	Britain
23. *Ghana*	Accra	30.4	West	3.6.1957	Britain
24. *Guinea*	Conakry	12.8	West	10.2.1958	France

25. Guinea-Bissau	Bissau	1.9	West	9.24.1973	Portugal
26. Kenya	Nairobi	52.6	E-Central	12.12.1963	Britain
27. Lesotho	Maseru	2.1	South	10.4.1966	Britain
28. Liberia	Monrovia	4.9	West	8.26.1847	------
29. Libya	Tripoli	6.8	North	12.24.1951	Britain
30. Madagascar	Antananarivo	27.0	SE-Island	6.26.1960	France
31. Malawi	Lilongwe	18.6	SE	7.6.1964	Britain
32. Mali	Bamako	16.7	West	9.22.1960	France
33. Mauritania	Nouakchott	4.5	NW	11.28.1960	France
34. Mauritius	Port Louis	1.3	SE-Island	3.12.1968	Britain
35. Morocco	Rabat	36.5	NW	6.30.1969	Spain
36. Mozambique	Maputo	30.3	SE	6.25.1975	Portugal
37. Namibia	Windhoek	2.5	SW	3.21.1990	S. Africa
38. Niger	Niamey	23.1	Central	8.3.1960	France
39. Nigeria	Abuja	200.9	West	10.1.1960	Britain
40. Rwanda	Kigali	12.6	E-Central	7.1.1962	Belgium
41. Sao Tome' & Principe'	Sao Tome'	.2	W- Island	7.12.1975	Portugal
42. Senegal	Dakar	16.3	West	4.4.1960	France
43. Seychelles	Victoria	.1	E-Island	6.29.1976	Britain
44. Sierra Leone	Freetown	7.8	West	4.27.1961	Britain
45. Somalia	Mogadishu	15.4	N- Central	7.1.1960	Britain
46. South Africa (Azania)	Pretoria, Cape Town, & Bloemfontein	58.6	South	5.31.1910	Britain
47. South Sudan	Juba	11.0	Northeast	7.9.2011	
48. Sudan	Khartoum	42.8	Northeast	1.1.1956	Britain
49. Tanzania	Dodoma	58.0	E-Central	12.9.1961	Britain
50. Togo	Lomé'	8.1	West	4.27.1960	France
51. Tunisia	Tunis	11.7	North	3.20.1956	France
52. Uganda	Kampala	44.3	E-Central	10.9.1962	Britain
53. Zambia	Lusaka	17.9	South	10.24.1964	Britain
54. Zimbabwe	Harare	14.7	South	4.18.1980	Britain

Section 2: IN ACTION

1. Name five of natural mineral resources that are abundant in Africa, that make it still a target for western control.

2. What are six waterways either within Africa or surrounding Africa?

1.	4.
2.	5.
3.	6.

3. *How map savvy are you?* Have participants complete as much of the map of Africa's countries as possible in 15 minutes. Then have them commit to add two more each week. You can make it a contest with small rewards. (See blank map on next page.)

4. Look up: Which countries in Africa became independent countries within the last 25 years? Which countries did they break away from?

Country....	Broke from...

Africa

Section 3

AFRICA

And the origins of life

Nyame nnwu na mawu:
perpetual existence

Highlights:

1. Africa, center of the world: Pangaea and Gondwanaland
2. The spread of biological life from an African center

Words Worth Heeding: *History is the landmark by which we are directed into the true course of life. The history of a movement, the history of a nation, the history of a race is the guidepost of that movement's destiny, that nation's destiny, that race's destiny.*

–Marcus M. Garvey

Africa In Time: The Origins of the World

All dates are approximate, based on scientific studies. This timeline only includes selected major historical occurrences.

20 billion years	Origin of the universe?
4.5 billion	Formation of the Earth
4.2 billion	Evidence of first rock formations
3.5 billion	First organic life, believed a single-celled creature; discovered in Figtree, Swaziland, AFRICA
600 million years ago	Existence of Pangaea (Earth as one land mass); AFRICA was at the center
200 million years ago	Existence of Gondwanaland (one of two supercontinents; enabling the spread of life from an AFRICAN center)
65 million years ago	South America breaks away from Africa, becoming a separate continent
50 million years ago	India collides with Asia, becoming a part of that continent
12 million years ago	Probable age of first hominids—human ancestors

Regarding the Earth's lands and people, Africa plays the most significant role in the dramatic story of the origins of life.

Check out your mind

1. Take a guess: How old do you guess the Earth is, based on scientists' theory? _____

2. Scientists believe the first life itself was a single-cell creature billions of years ago, based on fossils in Africa. What is a fossil?

   _____ _____

3. The theory of the continents being all connected with Africa at the center is called by a term that means "all lands." What is that term?

   _____ _____

While science plays a major role in our understanding and interpretation of ourselves and our world, far too many African American students approach this field with disinterest or trepidation. Since the Euro-centric view of science and history deliberately expunged the ground-breaking contributions of our Black African past from textbooks, our students' disinterest in these two areas is not all that surprising. In their role, scientists have been authorized to systematize the facts of history, discover, and define principles, and validate them through experimentation. They are key players in the allocation of power, especially as it relates to the dissemination of commonly held beliefs and concepts. Modern scientists have advanced many powerful theories that have improved human life; yet their blunders and biases (as we will address in the next few sections) have led to faulty, egregious lies and conclusions related to the role of Africa in history.

Africans were the original scientists, the true originators of medicine, astrology, astronomy, physics and more. Through their knowledge, early civilizations developed, flourished, and advanced. Today, African Americans are often the butt of negative scientific theories and experiments—theories which attempt to prove Black people are intellectually inferior, have smaller brain sizes, etc. And there are, for example, the 20th Century Tuskegee syphilis experiments (1930s) and the harvesting and cloning of the cells of Henrietta Lacks (1950s) for white profit and Black misery. Black students must be strongly encouraged to pursue scientific study and not fear it, recognizing they are capable of mastery and that their forebears were the original scientists.

Our understanding of our origins comes to us from members of various branches of science. These predominantly European scientists have given us theories and "facts" about the Earth's origin. It is up to us, however, to test these facts and to ascribe meaning to their observations. Their investigations into ancient history point to the centrality of Africa in the origin of life and humanity.

Scientific knowledge must become the domain of many, not the select few. Students and teachers of history need at least a working grasp in the fields of tectonics, archaeology, geology, and anthropology to lay the foundation for their study of African history—to find our ancient beginnings (millions of years ago, not 400 years ago on slave ships). Important clues to the origins of all things lie within these realms and can only be appreciated when one has, at minimum, conducted a cursory examination of these fields.

Africa plays the most significant role of the earth's lands and peoples in the story of origins. Africa holds the key to the existential questions that define our sense of self today: *Who am I? Who are we?* The following exploration of the science that undergirds these truths of Africa's primacy in the origins of all life, natural and human, helps establish a solid footing for our lives and enriches our appreciation for our African homeland.

Related Sciences

Anthropology: the study of humans and human ancestors, their societies, culture and development

Archaeology: the study of past human life utilizing the remains of ancient people, including their tools, artifacts and customs

Geology: study of the earth's crust, its layers and history.

Paleontology: the study of early life forms, as represented through fossil remains of animals and plants.

Africa, Origins and Center of the World

One of the mysteries of existence is how and when the universe came into being. If science is correct, the universe itself is quite old, and as it evolved, Africa was central to that development.

Origins of the Universe and Earth: Scientists now estimate the universe (the cosmos, all existence including matter and space as a whole) to be approximately 13.8 billion years old. Although theories differ as to how the cosmos came to exist, modern scientific findings place the age of the Earth at about four and a half billion years. The estimated age of the Earth has expanded over the last few centuries and innovations in science led to improved tools for measuring Earth's age. In 1650 a.d., Irish Bishop James Usher dated the world's beginning at 4004 b.c. This date, indicative of the limited knowledge of Europe's scholars during the Middle Ages, is inexcusably still listed in some bible chronologies, attempting to trace human generations back to the Bible's Genesis mythology of Adam and Eve's human origin.

In 1800 a.d., based on fossil evidence from French geologists who dispelled such a recent date as Usher's, the Earth was reassigned an age of 70,000 years. By 1830, scientists established the basis to date the Earth at millions of years old. Now, as noted, modern physicists commonly accept the estimation of 4.5 billion years old as the age of the beginning of the Earth.

Origins of Biological Life: Fossil records indicate *biological* life existed billions of years ago as well. Research from the late 20th Century indicates the first biological (animate) life emerged about 3.5 billion years ago at a site called Figtree near the Umbilizi River in Swaziland (southeast Africa). A Washington Post article reported research findings in November 1977: *"The seeds of life were first sown 3.5 billion years ago in a shallow swamp in Swaziland in the south of Africa."*

Seeds of Life Traced to Africa

3.5 Billion-Year-Old, 1-Cell Fossils

The Latest Clue to Origin of Species

By THOMAS O'TOOLE
Washington Post

The seeds of life were first sown 3.5 billion years ago in a shallow swamp in Swaziland in the south of Africa.

It is a place geologists call Figtree, where the waters of the Umhlati River wash through a rolling countryside on the way to Mozambique and the Indian Ocean.

Life began at Figtree as microscopic one-celled creatures that rapidly divided, then spread around the world by the winds

First in a Series

and evolved to form a soup of blue-green algae that persisted as the only life on Earth for more than two billion years.

These conclusions come from a Science magazine article by Harvard University paleontologist Elso Barghoorn, who says he found microscopic fossils at Figtree that go back 3.5 billion years.

"There may be fossils in other parts of the world older than Figtree," Barghoorn said in his laboratory at Harvard's Herbaria Museum, "but we haven't found any. So Figtree looks like the bottom of the pile."

Turn to Page 16A, Column 1

This original life is described by geologists as a single-celled creature, which spread around the world and evolved into a blue-green algae. (There have been claims since then that the first biological life may have emerged in other places but that is still viewed as conjecture.) What is clear is that it makes sense that the original life began in Africa because as we will see next is how scientists have confirmed over and over that life spread to the rest of the world from an African center.

The Swaziland discovery is doubly important because, not only was the first life in Africa, but in Africa's deepest reaches. There is little chance that Swaziland, in what's considered today as *blackest Africa* (about as far as one in Africa can get from Europe), can be removed from the continent and made a part of the Middle East or Europe, as was done with Egypt to discredit the discoveries proving the earliest civilizations were Black civilizations. Our children should know that even the very first life of any kind began in our Motherland—Africa.

Shifting Earth with Africa at the Center: Pangaea, Gondwanaland

Since the beginning of the Earth and life upon it, evidence points to the physical structure of the Earth dramatically and constantly shifting through a gradual process. Examining these changes helps explain the spread of life around the globe. What are considered today's *seven* (more accurately "six") continents were, in the Paleozoic Era (200-600 million years ago), one colossal land mass, which geologists named **Pangaea** (Greek for *all lands* or *whole earth*).

The waters of the Earth were likewise believed unified into one body termed **Panthalassa** (*all sea*). There is greater speculation and uncertainty about the state of the land masses prior to about 200 million years ago, but scientists have amassed plenty of evidence to support their postulation of a single land mass about that time period. An observation of the representation of this mass (see graphic below), shows Africa at the center. Scientists make no big deal of this, but the earnest student of African history knows there is critical meaning in such a revelation.

Africa, center of the world: Scientists' representations of Pangaea

beginning between 200 and 600 million years ago to the present day

225 million years ago

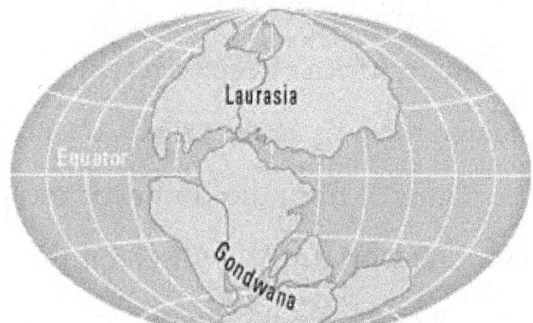

150 million years ago

Notice in the first model (225 million years ago) that Africa is at the center (and the same is true of all the succeeding scientific models). Notice the long strip of land on the left side of Africa which is today's North and South America; and Australia is on the right. These maps illustrate the steady shifting of the continents, allowing life to move out of Africa to other places.

100 million years ago

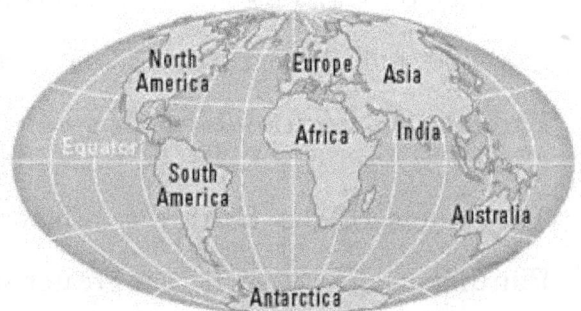

Earth today

If the continents once fit neatly into one land mass, how do scientists explain the present separation of this land mass into distinct continents? Scientists from the 19th Century developed the **continental drift** and **continental fit** theories to explain the present placement of the earth's land masses and activities in nature, such as earthquakes and volcanoes.

As shown in the Pangaea ("all lands") graphic, the continents once fit together (**continental fit**) into a single land mass, and over time began to drift apart; but not all at the same time. Some remained united for millions of years, while others drifted until they broke apart. **Continental drift**, then, refers to the gradual movement (i.e., drifting) of the continents, which are situated atop **tectonic plates**. Earth's land masses and oceans sit upon these plates, which are like giant rafts and form the crust of the Earth. There are believed to be seven *major* plates.

One version of a map of the shifting tectonic plates

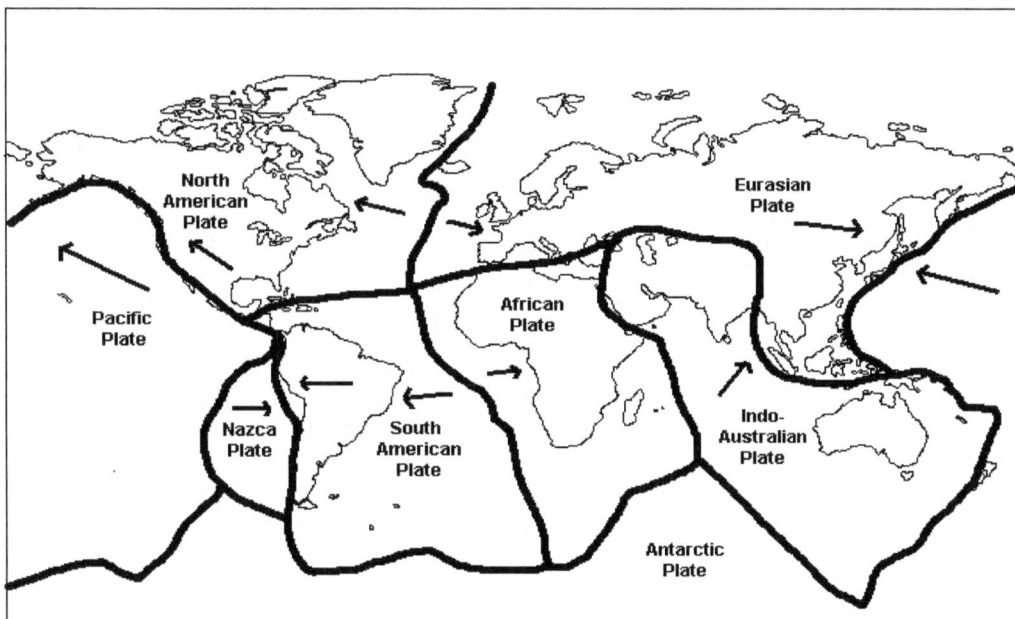

It is further speculated that these thick plates, the Earth's mantle (as illustrated in the graphic "a map of shifting tectonic plates" on previous page), were connected by dense strips of land, called **land bridges**. These linked the major masses of land together. Over thousands and even millions of years, as a result of the shifting of the tectonic plates, some of these land bridges sank into the oceans, allowing the masses of land to separate slowly. Today, after millions of years of movement, we have the familiar, distinguishable lands which are today's continents and islands.

This fascinating dialogue on the movement of these plates is addressed with great depth in texts related to geology and tectonics. For those seeking greater study in this area, among the most prominent of these pioneering geologists of the 19th and 20th Centuries are Eduard Suess, Antonio Snider, Alfred Wegener, and Alexander DuToit.

Some Terms

Continental drift: the slow movement of the earth's land masses caused by shifting tectonic plates.

Continental fit: describes how neatly some of the continents fit beside each other.

Fault: a break in the Earth's surface caused by shifting plates. Many ancient fossils are in faults.

Fossils: hardened remains or traces of an animal or plant preserved in the Earth's crust.

Tectonic plates: major slab-like sections that make up the structure of the Earth's crust.

Africa matters in all of this. When identical **fossils** were discovered during the 1800s in such distant places as southern Africa and India, scientists began to take note. These similarities in the fossilized plants and animals began to show up in increasing numbers. How could they explain the spread of plants and animals in parts of the world which are now separated by thousands of miles, even across oceans? Could plants somehow jump across vast bodies of water? Could land animals swim across thousands of miles of water? This was implausible, so the scientific community began to expand their understanding and interpretation of the spread of life out of Africa, by developing and testing the notion that the Earth's floor may have shifted.

Little did scientists realize they were helping reconstruct African history, which their colleagues in anthropology and anatomy were simultaneously disparaging, with their 18th and 19th Century treatises on Black inferiority (remember: they were deep in the throes of raping Africa for enslaved labor and natural resources). Nevertheless, their research indicates that about 200 million years ago, as a result of the constantly shifting plates beneath the Earth, Pangaea broke into two supercontinents— **Gondwanaland** and **Laurasia**. Gondwanaland is given the most attention because of the numerous fossils unearthed there, which help explain the spread of the earliest life, particularly throughout the southern hemisphere.

The Two Supercontinents. The southern supercontinent is called Gondwanaland and was much larger than Laurasia (North America and Eurasia). Gondwanaland included **South America, Australia, Antarctica, India, and Africa,** with the equator running through it.

As noted by scientists' reconstruction, Africa was at Gondwanaland's center—connected to more continents than any of the other continents. It is worth remembering that biological life had already begun in Africa and spread more rapidly to those areas in the closest proximity to it. Africa, we can conclude, was not only the center of the equatorial southern supercontinent, but this centrality made it possible for life forms to spread throughout what are today the Black and Brown regions of the world. It was that life that later spread to the north, where the climates were colder and less conducive for biological life.

Gondwanaland and Laurasia continued their drifting. And in a gradual process (over millions of years), the continents found their present positions. Diagrams of the reconstruction of continental fit show that the east coast of South America fits neatly with the west coast of Africa (see graphic "The Two Supercontinents" on next page). **Mountain ranges in Brazil have been matched with ranges in Nigeria, to form one continuous range**.

The study of the Earth's shifting plates explains the existence of some of the Earth's other structural features. **Faults** (breaks in the Earth's surface) are the result of the shifting of the tectonic plates. Scientists unearth ancient remains of the living and nonliving past where the fault lines meet. Structural features such as mountain ranges and mid-ocean ridges are produced as a result of the shifting of the Earth's floor.

Two Supercontinents: Gondwanaland and Laurasia

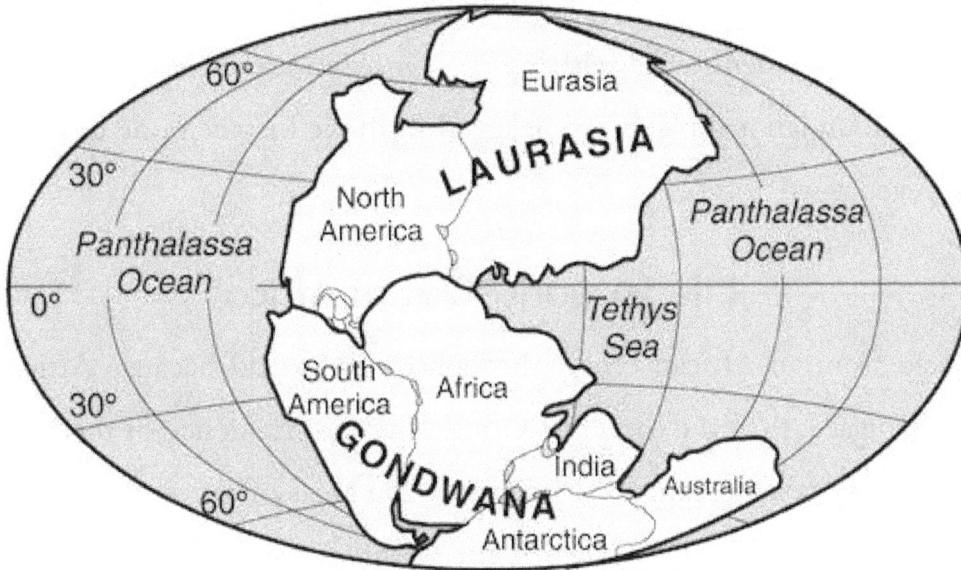

Scientists Timetable for Major Shifts of Land Masses

200 million years ago	Pangaea separates into two supercontinents
165 million years ago	North America separates from Africa
65 million years ago	South America breaks from Africa
50 million years ago	India collides with Asia Australia begins detaching from Antarctica
18-16 million years ago	Africa joins Eurasia
2 million years ago	South America joined North America

Unstable areas (those where earthquakes and volcanoes occur, e.g., the Rift Valley in East Africa and along the California coastline) lie along plate boundaries, created by tectonic plate movements. They either *move apart, move toward (colliding), or slide past each other.* These foundational plates are believed to move between one and four inches annually, even now!

Life Spreads "Out of Africa"

Life spread from an African center throughout the world because Africa was the center of Pangaea, then the center of Gondwanaland. Evidence of this includes the discovery of animal and plant fossils unearthed in areas of the world where they can no longer thrive. What this confirmed for scientists was that the continents must have been situated differently than they are today.

Examples of continental fit and the spread of life (see graphic on next page) include discovery of fossils of the **Mesosaurus** (a freshwater reptile) found in both South Africa and South America, dating over 100 million years. **Lystrosaurus** (a hippopotamus) remains have been found in Africa, India, and Antarctica. The remains of **Glossopteris** (a fernlike plant) were found in South America, India, Africa, and Australia.

Many Old and New World primates (*a class of mammals with advanced brains, hands, feet, etc.*) traveled from Africa throughout the world. Scientists support the idea of the spread of life "out of Africa" by reminding us that had these lands not been in very close proximity, these life forms would not have survived in the locations where the fossils were found.

Fossil evidence of the Triassic land reptile Lystrosaurus.

Fossil remains of Cynognathus, a Triassic land reptile approximately 3m long.

Fossil remains of the freshwater reptile Mesosaurus.

Fossils of the fern Glossopteris, found in all of the southern continents, show that they were once joined.

AFRICA

INDIA

SOUTH AMERICA

ANTARTICA

AUSTRALIA

Spread of life from the Gondwanaland, southern supercontinent. Gondwanaland is a significant piece of the history of African people and the whole of humanity. It provides a starting point. For Black people, a displaced and disparaged people, this linkage is profound. These are primal roots, the beginning; a point of origin reaching back into a million millennia.

The Gondwanaland history is the beginning of reconnecting a fragmented lineage, a key point in recovering our fragmented identity. The need for African-centered or at minimum African-infused education is no idle notion, nor is it an issue of simply affirming the worth of students in predominantly Black school systems. While it is key to their healthy emotional, social, and political development, it is **historically correct** for all peoples because Africa is the center and point of origin for all existence, and that is according to the world's pre-eminent scientists.

Section 3: IN ACTION

1. **How much do you recall? Match the five items below by drawing a line to the corresponding answer.**

1. Oldest life form was found in…	Panthalassa
2. The southern supercontinent from which life spread was called…	Archaeology
3. One area that studies ancient life…	Swaziland
4. Approximate age of the universe…	Gondwanaland
5. The term used to describe when all the bodies of water were unified as one…	13.8 billion years

2. **Sit in a group and read aloud and discuss the following quote about the purpose of history.**

   History should tell a people who they are, where they came from and what their potential is as a people. If it fails to do so, it is useless.[13]

   Use these questions to make personal meaning of the quote.

   1. How has the history to which you have been exposed accomplished or not accomplished these ideas?

   2. What 1-2 things could we do to make history more meaningful and empowering for our children and communities?

---

[13] Browder, A. *Nile Valley contributions to civilization*, p. 30

Section 4

AFRICA

And the origins of humanity

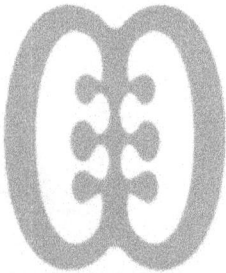

Ese ne tekrama
We improve and advance;
also interdependence

Highlights:

1. Futile search for human origins outside of Africa
2. Africa, the cradle of humanity
3. The first humans were socially cooperative

Words Worth Heeding: *The hard fact is that most of what we now call world history is only the history of the first and second rise of Europe.... The history of Africa was already old when Europe was born.* —John Henrik Clarke

Africa and the Origin of Humanity

Out of Africa: The Road to Modern Humans

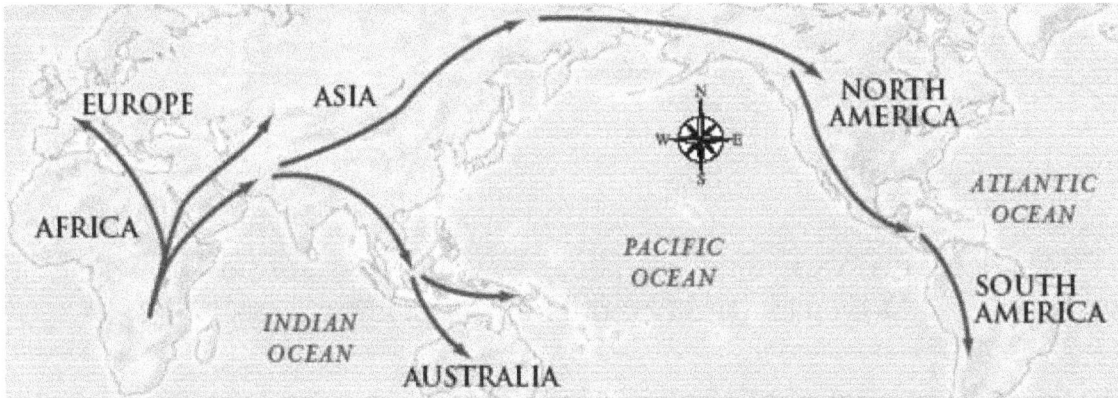

The **OUT OF AFRICA** model is consistent with fossil evidence; homo sapiens emerged in Africa, then spread to the rest of the world. Eurocentric scientists are fighting, to this day, to disprove this truth. **All dates are scientists' approximations.**

12 million years ago	*1ˢᵗ of the hominid, human-like species (Ramapithecus) in Africa*
4 million years ago **Early humans**	**The first of the *homo* line begins in Africa**; food gathering, standing upright, and early tool use (Australopithecus) including key fossil findings dated 3.75- 1.5 million years: *Tanzania, 1975, Leakey; Lucy of Hadar, Ethiopia; Zinjanthropus Boisei in 1959 and 1961, Leakeys; Homo erectus, homo habilis*
130,000 – 200,000 **Modern humans**	***First homo sapiens and homo sapiens sapiens: modern humans*** *(Omo, Ethiopia; Laetoli, Tanzania, Klasies River Mouth and Border Cave, South Africa*
115,000-130,000 or earlier	*Humans are believed to have begun moving out from Africa to other parts of the world; some believe the move out of Africa was earlier*
40,000 **Metal processing**	*Evidence of African societies **processing metals** (for tools and weapons)*
8,000 b.c. **Agriculture**	***Agricultural Era*** *began in Africa, laying the foundation for the rise of civilization from Africa out into the rest of the world.*

Even with an ever-changing definition of what constitutes "human," Africa is the undisputed birthplace of ancient and modern humans.

Check out your mind

1. There are two views (models) about how humanity spread throughout the world. Do you know either or both? Name them.

   _____   _____

2. Name two locations in Africa where the earliest human fossils were discovered.

   _____   _____

3. A lot of effort was undertaken to not give credit to humanity's origin in Africa. What is one of the popular stories about humanity beginning in Europe or Asia?

   _____

M oving from Gondwanaland, along a historical time continuum, the study of world and human development continues to be centered in Africa. An accurate chronology makes clear the primacy of Africa in human origins and development. This section helps ground us in a pride-filled, healthy identity as people of African descent.

Without a doubt, humanity began in Africa, in its interior (the so-called "darkest Africa"). Despite the persistent efforts of European academics to discredit Africa, countless discoveries have been unearthed to shatter their lies. Excavations of the first humans were made in various areas of Africa.

The oldest fossils of humans were found throughout three major areas:

1) The Great Lakes Region of central east Africa

2) Ethiopia

3) southern Africa

According to anthropologists, humans are nearly four (4) million years old and lived in an atmosphere of social cooperation. There are no comparative fossils of human remains in Europe or Asia that date even close to those unearthed in Africa. Nonetheless, Eurocentrists did not accept these truths easily.

Search for Human Origins Outside Africa

Since the 16th Century, when the brutal European exportation of enslaved Africans into the Americas began, there has been an unyielding effort to crush and discredit any scientific findings that shed a positive light on Africa and African people. This malevolent conspiracy permeated every academic discipline, including archaeology.

European treatises espousing the racial inferiority of Black people in defense of the system of African enslavement came into direct conflict with a series of natural science discoveries over a 100-year period. Between 1859 and 1959, the combination of these discoveries would shatter the ideological foundation upon which a general declaration of Black inferiority was constructed.

The first discovery pointing to an African origin of humanity was made by Charles Darwin, famed naturalist from England. He spent five years (1831 to 1836) on a ship that sailed around the world. He was the ship's naturalist. In that capacity, he collected and studied a massive amount of shells, plants, animal, and human fossils. Upon returning to England, he studied his notes from the journey and the specimens he collected. Darwin concluded that there was a common descent of all species. His *theory of common descent* asserted that each life species, including humans, descended from a common ancestry.

In the mid-1800s, Charles Darwin concluded that Africa is the cradle of humanity.

In 1859, Darwin's theories of common descent first appeared in his book, *The Origin of Species by Means of Natural Selection*. In a later book[14], Darwin reached two monumental conclusions with implications that would take nearly 100 years to fully unravel. One of the ideas of great importance to this discussion, was his conclusion that the African continent is the cradle of humanity—the historical "Garden of Eden." This thesis was based upon reasoning that in every region of the world the extant mammals (those still present today) were closely related to extinct (phased out) species from the same region, and that region was Africa. Darwin further concluded that it is most likely that humanity's predecessors lived in Africa, rather than any other part of the world.

---

[14] Darwin, C. 1871. *The descent of man and selection in relation to sex.*

Discoveries since then proved Darwin correct and indicate that at **every stage of development and adaptation to the environment up to and including, the beginning of modern humans took place in Africa.**

Prior to Darwin's writings, archaeologists had focused their search for human beginnings primarily in Europe, then exasperated they turned to Asia. It was inconceivable, in the minds of Europeans engaged in the subjugation of so-called inferior Africans, that their own origins could have been in Black Africa. In 1856, fossils of early human predecessors' skulls were discovered in Germany in the Neander Valley, not by archaeologists but by limestone workers. These bones were classified as Neanderthal Man, who lived between 30,000 and 100,000 years ago.

At every stage of development and adaptation, up to and including, the beginning of modern humans took place in Africa.

In France, during 1868, workmen unearthed remains of five fossil groupings that had physical structures like modern humans. These remains were found in a rock shelter and were labeled Cro-Magnon Man. Then, at some point between 1891 and 1898 in Java, Indonesia, a Dutch naturalist discovered a skull cap and a leg bone of a species that was somewhere between man and ape, termed Java Man. It is not all that ironic that these are the few pre-human or humanlike fossils we learned about in U.S. schools. As will be shown, these were not "modern humans" nor the oldest fossils. The first human were in Africa, even though this is not a standard feature of today's science curricula. This is another example of the lengths taken to erase Africa's historical significance and advance the centrality of Europe in all that is worthwhile.

In 1924, Raymond Dart, a professor of anatomy in South Africa, made a fossil find that would shift the search for human origins away from Asia and Europe and into Africa. Dart, at a place called Taung in southern Africa, discovered the remains of a being which was neither ape nor human (an early member of the human lineage, estimated at 2.3-2.8 million years old). Dart's Taung fossil called *australopithecus africanus* supported Darwin's view that the earliest humans would be unearthed in Africa.

Then in 1938, Robert Broom unearthed more remains of a *hominid* (of the highest order of mammals in the human line) in South Africa that lived approximately three million years ago. These discoveries were not given much attention initially, but over time, as more fossils were found in Africa, the excavation crews began moving their camps to Africa. Over the next 25 years, **southern Africa became the prime location for the search for fossil remains related to human origins.** Some of the major excavation sites in modern-day South Africa included: Taung, Kromdraai, Border Cave, Klasies River, Swartkrans, and Sterfontein.

1859-1959- SHIFTING THE SEARCH FOR HUMANITY TO AFRICA

1859: Charles Darwin Common Descent Theory, Africa cradle of humanity

1868: Cro-Magnon Man, France

1891/98: Java Man, Indonesia

1912: Piltdown Forgery, England

1924: Raymond Dart, Taung discovery, S. Africa

1938: Robert Broom, hominid discovery, S. Africa

1959: Leakey's discovery, E. Africa, Africa cradle of humanity

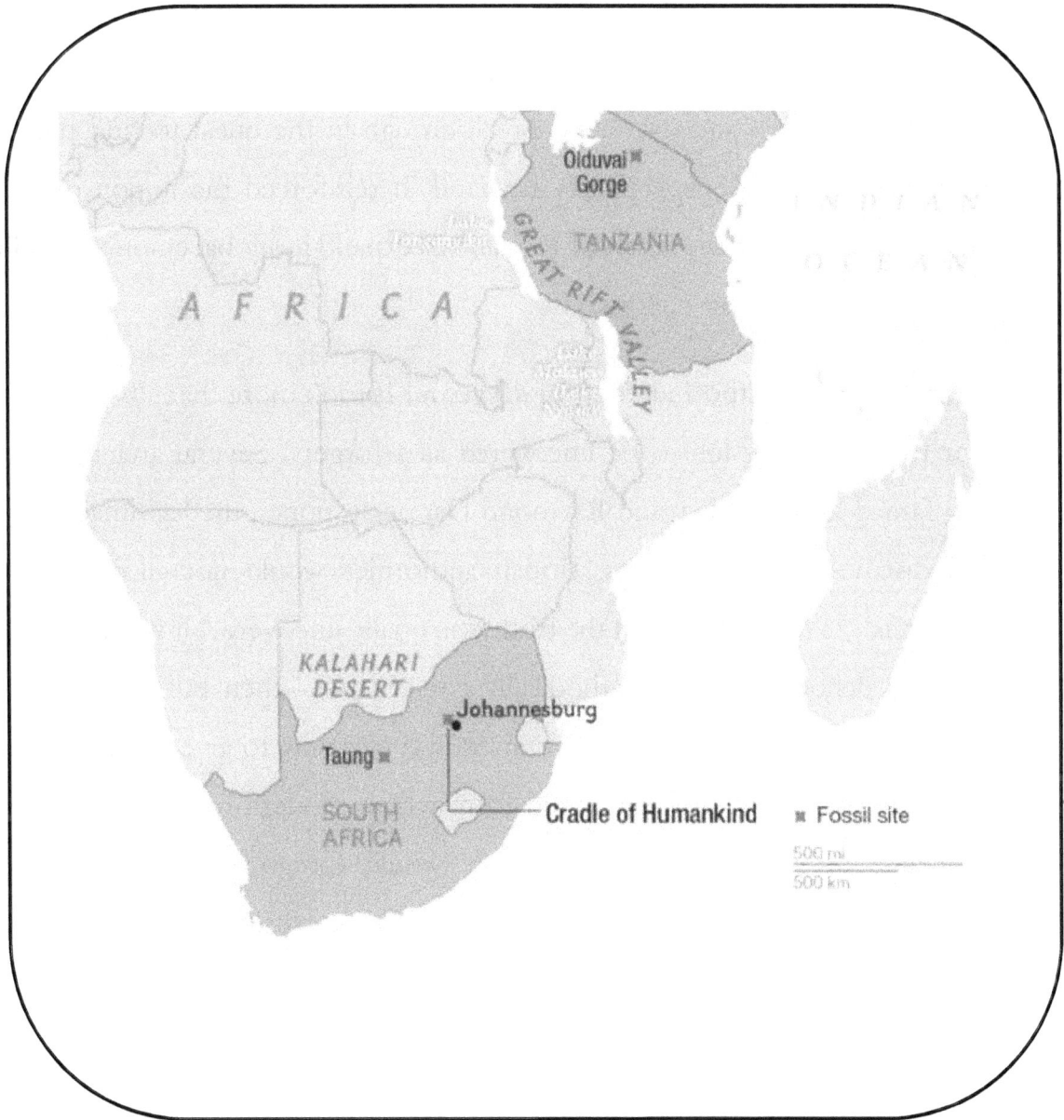

England's Piltdown Man- A Forgery. The discoveries by Dart and Broom were initially discounted by European archaeologists for two reasons. First, Europeans refused to believe that humanity's descendants (including theirs) began in Africa.

Second, they found relief from that idea through the efforts of an amateur British archaeologist named Charles Dawson in 1912. His pivotal find was of a hominid skull in a grave in southern England, labeled the **Piltdown Man**. The discovery was received enthusiastically and deemed a breakthrough in the quest to find the first modern human in Europe, specifically England. It reinforced the notion of white and Anglo supremacy and the effort of England to expand its global empire including dominating other European nations.

An egregious lie that stood as fact for 40 years! It took more than 40 years, until 1955, for the Piltdown Man to be uncovered as a forgery. Several archaeologists, including famed Louis Leakey and Raymond Dart, questioned the legitimacy of the Piltdown discovery. But for years, British authorities would not allow them to thoroughly analyze the skull. When the truth was finally uncovered, it was found that someone had deliberately and methodically constructed—then buried—a human cranium along with the jaw of an orangutan in that gravesite to give the appearance that they were the remains of a hominid from which modern humans descended. Are we really surprised that these scientists would forego ethical standards to fabricate this forgery? This case is emblematic of the pattern of white western scientific tampering, with which we are familiar. Leakey reminds us of this tendency:

> *The Piltdown forgery illustrates the sometimes indecent eagerness with which scientists will accept what they want to believe…At a time when much of the scientific world was still seduced by the Piltdown forgery, the discovery (1924) of*

a supposed human fossil in such a remote and basically 'barbaric' land as South Africa was treated with contempt and scorn...[15] P. 33

Africa, Cradle of Humanity

Along with Dart and Broom, Louis Leakey and his wife Mary were convinced that Darwin was correct—Africa was the place of human origins. The Leakeys, British archaeologists, beginning in 1926, searched for human origins in eastern Africa at sites in modern-day Kenya and Tanzania along the Rift Valley. After decades of meticulous work, in July 1959, 100 years after Charles Darwin argued for an African origin of humanity, the Leakeys made a defining fossil discovery. It would shake loose the ideological notion undergirding the power of white western culture—the fallacy of white primacy in the story of the origins of humanity. These fossils indicated all humanity descended from Black Africa.

The Leakey era of fossil discovery: On that July day, Mary Leakey found a complete skull of an ancient human ancestor. This intact cranium was labeled *Australopithecus boisei* (originally called *zinjanthropus boisei or eastern man*). This was a watershed moment in that it was the first hominid that was dated properly, prompting droves of scientists to redirect their search for humanity's birthplace to East Africa. The remains were of one who lived approximately 1.75 million years ago in Tanzania's Olduvai Gorge area.

---

[15] Leakey R.E. and Lewin, L. 1992. *Origins revisited.*

Two years later, in 1961, the Leakeys came upon the oldest fossil remains of true humans (termed *"homo"* from which all modern humans descended) also at the Olduvai Gorge. Measurement instruments indicated these humans lived at the same time as those from the hominid lineage discovered in 1959.

Then in 1972, the Leakeys, digging in Kenya around Lake Turkana, discovered the oldest complete skull of homo habilis (*skilled* humans; users of crude tools to manage and engage with their environment), dated at 1.75 to 2.0 million years as well. Also related, in 1975, again at Lake Turkana, the most complete skull of *homo erectus* (one with a fully upright spine) was found by a member of the Leakey team, the most recent ancestor of modern humans. It was dated 1.5 million years old. Additionally, in 1975, the Leakeys uncovered fossils which may indicate early human ancestors began nearly four million years ago. These were characterized by their fully bipedal carriage (referring to walking on two feet, fully upright) and food gathering practices—marvels of human adaptation to their changing external environment. Richard Leakey, son of Louis and Mary, in *Origins* states:

> *…spectacular fossils, found particularly by Don Johanson…in the arid wastes of Ethiopia, but also by Mary Leakey…in the long-neglected fossil bearing deposits a few miles from Olduvai Gorge, include examples of primitive homo erectus four million years old. P. 88*

Man Traced 3.75 Million Years By Fossils Found in Tanzania

By Boyce Rensberger Special to The New York Times

Oct. 31, 1975   f y ✉ ↗

The Leakeys' fossil discoveries (and those of others) are evidence that *homo erectus*, the closest ancestor to modern humans (*homo sapiens*) emerged first and exclusively in Africa. Homo erectus, having developed a more sophisticated social culture was able to eventually migrate into other areas of the world. Around one half million years ago, this species is believed to have evolved into modern humans (*homo sapiens*) and, about 100,000-200,000 years ago into the current more sophisticated human species, termed *homo sapiens sapiens*.

More recent discoveries support the thesis that even these later human developments first took place on the continent of Africa. Diop's *Civilization or Barbarism* provides a review of the dates that *homo sapiens sapiens* appeared in different parts of the world. His reports, consistent with other researchers, are that this modern human originated in Africa, at Omo River and other African sites and was dated approximately 150,000 years ago.

Out of Africa Model Obliterates Multiregional Model

These numerous African fossil finds dealt another blow to racist academics, who had made sense of the African finds by putting forth the idea that only *primitive* humans originated in Africa. They went to great lengths to build a case that modern "intelligent" human had their origins elsewhere.

One popular theory, known as the **Coonian Thesis**, had begun circulating in support of this flawed view beginning in the 1960s. Carleton Coon's theory held that *homo erectus* (early human) left Africa and went in five different directions. Then, at some point later, homo erectus evolved into modern humans outside of Africa. A careful look at this premise reveals another crack in the racist analyses of the fossil record, in that it postulated that Africans never evolved to full (i.e., real) humans, or at least if they did, it was much later than groups outside of Africa. Dr. Charles Finch, an African American historian states[16]:

> In fact, Coon categorically declared: 'Africa is the birthplace of the human race, but it is only the undifferentiated kindergarten. Europe and Asia were our principal school.' There was more: a racial hierarchy was devised based on the skull size and shape where Coon placed the Asiatic and European at the top and the African type at the bottom. Pp. 12-13

By the 1990s, this argument was rendered untenable after three more significant fossil finds were reported. These fossils were of homo sapiens and homo sapiens sapiens (modern humans). They were discovered during the 1970s and 1980s in Omo, Ethiopia; Laetoli, Tanzania; Klasies River Mouth, South Africa; and Border Cave, South Africa, ranging between 130,000 and 200,000 years old. No other modern human skulls of this age have been found anywhere else in the world. American journalists have reported on these discoveries and their possible implications. The *New York Times reported* on this breakthrough in 2005:

> Scientists have determined that human fossils found in Ethiopia in 1967 are 65,000 years older than first thought, from about 195,000 years ago. The revised date, they said, makes the skulls and bones the earliest known remains of modern homo sapiens. The research reinforces the theories of an African origin for modern humans.[17]

---

[16] Finch III, C. S. 1991. *Echoes of the old darkland: Themes from the African Eden*. Khenti, Inc
[17] Wilford, J. N. Feb. 16, 2005. Oldest remains of human beings identified. *New York Times*.

These discoveries had meaning for the two competing models of the birth of modern humans, the "multiregional" model and the "Out of Africa" model. The first of the two, multiregional model, as already mentioned, claims that homo erectus (near human) left Africa and spread across the world, after which time and in various locations, modern humanity emerged, namely in Europe and Asia.

The "Out of Africa" model, based on the scientific fossil record, shatters the "multiregional model" in that **modern humans emerged first in Africa**, and in areas today considered Black Africa. These, brainy and cultured people lived in the southernmost reaches of Africa, prior to any emergence or arrival into any of the other areas of the world. This model argues that this modern African human group spread throughout the world—a **wonderful early Diaspora** (dispersion) that populated the earth! Africa was the birthplace of the first humans in each stage of humanity's development.

Martin Meredith, in *Born in Africa: The Question for the Origins of Human Life*[18], summarizes this conversation about Africa as the source of human life:

> *Scientists have identified more than 20 species of extinct humans. They have firmly established Africa is the birthplace not only of humankind but also modern humans. They have revealed how early technology, language ability, and artistic endeavor all originated in Africa, and they have shown how small groups of Africans possessing new skills, spread out from Africa in an exodus 60,000 years ago to populate the rest of the world. We have all inherited an African past. P. xiv*

---

[18] Meredith, M. 2012.

It is also noteworthy that scientists indicate **humans are not descended from apes**. The human predecessors and modern humans co-existed and still do—alongside the primate group to which monkeys, apes and orangutans belong.

Africa is our true Garden of Eden. As we have briefly described, all evidence—paleontological, anthropological and genetic—points to Africa as the point of origin of the human species. That evidence validates the single origin hypothesis—that all humans descended from a single pair of humans located on the continent of Africa, making them the mythological "Adam and Eve" in the "Garden of Eden."

Humans have searched for evidence of the origins of humanity and developed stories to explain and describe that first couple. Creation myths were developed during a period when there was no knowledge about either evolution or the emergence of homo sapiens. These myths compensated for the lack of scientific information that existed during the time they were written.

Nearly every religious tradition has a mythological story of human creation. Many religions, in their description of an unknown beginning contain elements paralleling those in the Adam and Eve story; some were written long before, others after. These ""myths" are tradition and culturally-based. Each attempts to address the mystery of how, where and by whom existence began.

This extensive body of fossil discoveries enables a convergence of science with religion by placing the mythical Garden of Eden, the first human couple's home, in Africa. As shared by Martin Meredith, modern geneticists began to establish DNA evidence to augment the African origins of the first family theory. In 1987, a team of biochemists from University of California-Berkley presented a research paper that provided further evidence that the modern human family derived from a single genetic line within Africa approximately 200,000 years ago[19]. Their research focused solely on women and pointed to the logic of an African Eve. They concluded that all present-day humans are descendants from that "Eve" in Africa. The possible locations of this "Eve" could have been Ethiopia or in southeast Africa.

Black young people must know the historical truth that Africa was the epicenter of human origins—the mythological "Garden of Eden." These statements are not wishful thinking; they are grounded in the facts of Africa's history. Africa is where the first humans emerged and where the earliest civilizations were spawned.

First Humans were Socially Cooperative, not Barbaric

Equally compelling is that the world's first families (in Africa) were socially advanced. When we think of civilized when compared with barbarism, descriptions include such elements as shared social structures and cultural features come to mind. The presence of arts, sciences, social norms, governance systems, etc., also generally characterize a higher state of social development.

Michael Bradley in his acclaimed *Iceman Inheritance* surmises that the rate and nature of the **development of humans** was highly contingent upon the physical environment with which the species had to cope and adapt. Africa as the geographic center of human life enabled humanity's development, adaptation and maturation at a more rapid pace than would have occurred elsewhere. It is both remarkable and significant that the Leakeys discovered through analysis of the African fossils that the original human families were not violent, as many had assumed, but were

---

[19] Meredith, M. 2012. *Out of Africa.*

cooperative. Richard Leakey, during a conference held in 1977, told his audience that his research indicated violence is a learned behavior, and it can be educated out. He based this view on his study of the African fossils of the first humans, and he made the following profound announcement about this first family:

> *Man is by nature cooperative, rather than aggressive...There is not a single*
> *fossil among 300 specimens I have that shows any sign of aggression or violence.*
> *Early man tracing back 2.5 million years was a hunter-gatherer—these*
> *communities still exist and can be observed. Their strongest characteristic is*
> *social cooperation.* [20]

These original humans lived in groups, shared their food, and protected each other. This was the principal criteria for drawing a distinction between the Australopithecines and true humans (homo). These fossils were free of signs of assault and attack, while some fossils from earlier species showed evidence of nicks

"Their strongest characteristic is social cooperation."

and skull indentations. The practice of hunting and gathering inclined these early families to learn to function as groups and practice social cooperation and what we would call Ujamaa— "cooperative economics." They learned to solve their problems together because they recognized their need for interdependence if they were to effectively engage their external environment and secure what they needed to live. This mature lifestyle was what distinguished the *hominids* from the *homo* line and was prevalent almost three million years ago. The !Kung people of southern Africa are

---

[20] Seabrook, C. Is man innately violent?, *The Atlanta Journal Constitution*, March 24, 1977, A3.

still studied today because they are considered an extant representation of this communal, harmonious lifestyle.

This news of early Africans' communal, cooperative lifestyle is important for African American students and adults. Not only do we need to know our ancestors were the first group of humans, confirming solid placement, rooting us in space and time, but also that **as a people altruism was encoded as a means to survive and thrive**. The tendency towards rugged individualism and violence is, as Leakey shared, learned behavior. Unlike what has been depicted in movies and textbooks—that early Africans were violent savages—our children need to know that their ancestors were, in fact, a mature collection of families who solved the challenges of life together.

Besides this discovery about the "nature" of the primal humans, the other central issue in all of this is that *modern* humans emerged in Africa, with all the characteristics described for *homo sapiens*. These early humans paved the way for more advanced communal cultures and civilizations along the Nile River. Africa provided the ideal physical environment for the progression of primal humans into sophisticated, communal families. In 100 years (1859-1959) of archaeology, natural science, and anthropology, the western world's declaration of the inferiority of Africa and her offspring was decimated. And with the efforts of modern-day African Diasporan historians, the remaining vestiges of that narrative will continue losing potency.

In summary, the primal communal cultures that emerged among the original families in Africa were harbingers of the ingenuity and innovation that would follow wherever they traveled. We turn now to the African origin of civilization in the next section.

Section 4: IN ACTION

1. List Five Fossil Facts (from this section). They can be places, definitions, dates, or names. Then compare and discuss with your group why everyone selected what they did.

   1. _____

   2. _____

   3. _____

   4. _____

   5. _____

2. What are 1-2 other negative perceptions about Africa that have been promoted in American society?

   _____

   _____

3. In groups, talk through 2-3 ways you can help shift to more positive perceptions of our Motherland. List them here.

   _____

   _____

   _____

   _____

Section **5**

AFRICA

The Nile Valley Origins of Civilization

Afena
*(a state ceremonial
sword)*
Recognition of gallantry

Highlights:

1. The attempt to de-Africanize Egypt
2. First civilization came from Nubia, south of Egypt

Words Worth Heeding: *We must recognize the intimate relationship between culture, history and personality. If we do not know our history, then we do not know our personality. And if the only history we know is other people's history then our personality has been created by that history.* –Amos N. Wilson

A sampling of Nile Valley Contributions

Architecture

Surgery and Pharmacology

Dentistry

Sciences: Chemistry, biology, engineering, astronomy, astrology

Papyrus: Writing paper

Mummification, Embalming and preserving

Irrigation systems

Domestication of animals

Government system

Cosmetology, Shaving

Mathematics, geometry, algebra, trigonometry, calculus

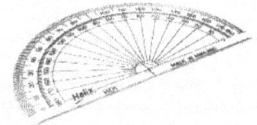

Monotheism, religious systems

Paved streets

Calendar: 365 1/4 day solar

Literature: Poetry, songs, fiction

Pulleys

Hieroglyphics: A writing system using pictures

Greece was the daughter of Africa's Nile Valley civilizations, not the originator of civilization, as asserted by white historians.

Check out your mind

1. Why and when did it become important for European historians to present Egypt as NOT a part of Africa?

   _____

2. The Nile River flows through several African countries enabling ancient civilizations to flourish. Name three of those countries.

   _____

3. What is the name of one ancient African Nile Valley civilization (besides Egypt)?

   _____

The preeminent Black scholar of the 20th Century, W.E.B. DuBois, in his classic book, *The World and Africa*, discusses the white fabrication of history. He points out that it was in East Africa's Nile Valley "*that the most significant continuous human culture arose*" (p. 98). DuBois also makes clear that, by borrowing from Egypt, the Greeks developed the first civilization in Europe (long after these early African civilizations had emerged and were flourishing). Europeans, however, could not psychologically accept such an idea—that their civilization had African origins. So, European historians manufactured a history that erased the African origins of European civilization. Says DuBois:

> *It is one of the astonishing results of the written history of Africa, that almost unanimously in the nineteenth century, Egypt was not regarded as part of Africa. Its history and culture were separated from that of the other inhabitants of Africa; it was even asserted that Egypt was in reality, Asiatic. P. 99*

Attempts to De-Africanize Egypt

With the many excavations revealing the existence of advanced ancient civilization and social structures in Egypt, de-Africanizing Egypt became a major focus of European historians during the 19th Century. What is important about this entire process is that up until that time, the majority of whites understood that the civilization of Greece had its origins by way of the spread of civilization from ancient Egypt (Bernal, *Black Athena*). This Africa-as-the-origin of Greek civilization perspective was the foundation of historical study until the 19th Century. It was at this same point in time that every effort was made to preempt this truth with a concocted tale of Greece as the place of the world's first civilization. As noted in Section 4, this is also the approximate timeframe when Darwin declared Africa the cradle of humanity—at odds with white scholars who rejected the ancient (African) model of history. This de-Africanizing of Egypt was no simple reimagining of history—it was a part of the white western world's aggressive campaign to grow its global power and influence. This Eurocentric

Recreating the flow and interpretation of historical events is a privilege of the

model was a foundational element for achieving that objective. Recreating the flow and interpretation of historical events is a privilege of the powerful!

Martin Bernal subtitled his first volume of *Black Athena*, "The Fabrication of Ancient Greece, 1785-1985." Bernal's position, like DuBois's, was that European civilization is an extension of Greece, and the Greeks built their culture upon African cultural and ideological foundations. Bernal, as addressed in Section I, defined this perspective of an African-originated civilization, as the *ancient model*. As noted earlier, the 19th Century witnessed the emergence of the *Eurocentric (or Aryan) model*, one asserting a northern European start of civilization. The claim was that there had been an invasion from the northern areas of Europe into Greece which destroyed the preHellenic (i.e., primitive) Greek culture. Allegedly, these plundering invaders from the north were ultimately the source of Greek civilization. The Aryan model removes any trace of African influence on the development of Greek civilization. The advance from primitivism to civilization in Europe had been turned into a purely white feat.

DuBois in an explanation as to why white historians began to separate Egypt from Africa, stated:

> *There can be but one adequate explanation of this vagary of the nineteenth century science: It was due to the fact that the rise and support of capitalism*

called for rationalization based upon degrading and discrediting the Negroid

people. P. 99

The process of restoring the ancient, fact-based, model of history begins with the exploration of the African origins of humanity, which was the central theme of Section 4. The reader was reminded that an early human-like primate species first became human (homo) in the east African Rift Valley. We now turn our attention briefly to the geography of the Nile Valley in our quest to clarify that the ancient Egyptians were Black Africans.

Geography of the Nile Valley. The Nile Valley is the abundantly fertile area that runs alongside all the lakes and tributaries that produce the Nile River. Many nations made their livelihood along the Nile. Several rivers flowing through Burundi, Rwanda and Tanzania provide some of the water that ultimately becomes the White Nile in southern Sudan. In the Sudanese city of Khartoum, the Blue and White Niles converge and flow northward, emptying into the Mediterranean Sea. The Nile River is the longest river in the world at 4,100 miles.

The Nile passes through, what are today, 11 different African countries. The Nile River, especially with its annual overflow, is central to life in these countries. With the seasonal overflow, deposits of silt and nutrient-rich soil, made for natural, high quality fertilizer for all the land adjacent to the Nile. Thus, the Nile provided our early African communities water, a means of transportation and agricultural abundance, in other words, a stable quality of life.

The Nile River Valley

Mediterranean Sea

Alexandria

Cairo

Nile

LIBYA

EGYPT

Luxor

Aswan

Lake Nasser

Red Sea

CHAD

Khartoum

SUDAN

ERITREA

Blue Nile

Lake Tana

CENTRAL
AFRICAN
REPUBLIC

SOUTH
SUDAN

White Nile

ETHIOPIA

Juba

*Lake
Albert*

UGANDA

Lake Kyoga

DEMOCRATIC
REPUBLIC
OF THE CONGO

Jinja

KENYA

RWANDA

BURUNDI

Lake Victoria

TANZANIA

Located in eastern, central, and northern Africa, the countries along the Nile River are:

- Burundi
- Dem. Rep. of Congo
- Eritrea (newer country)
- Ethiopia

- Egypt
- Kenya
- Rwanda
- South Sudan (newly independent country)

- Sudan
- Tanzania
- Uganda

First Civilization Came from *South* of Egypt

Gaining a historically accurate understanding of *who* the ancient Egyptians were means being clear that the *Nile River flows from south to north* and empties into the Mediterranean Sea. It is commonly known that people tend to migrate in the direction of the flow of rivers. Consequently, as the earliest primate species in Africa's Nile Valley developed into what is considered modern humanity (homo sapiens sapiens) in Africa, they also continued innovating, moving from hunting and gathering groups to small, agriculturally based cooperative communities. As documented in Section 4, in these communities, the early families and groups cultivated food and were noted for having a communal lifestyle (a culture of interdependency and sharing).

We should also be reminded that, according to Michael Bradley (*Iceman Inheritance*), as these early humans spread up, over and northward out of Africa, harsh environmental influences led them, Europeans in particular, to become more primitive and antagonistic in their behavior towards each other.

When these early African communities grew to a point that it put stress upon their land in central east Africa's Nile River area, small groups of people began to migrate in the direction of the flow of the Nile River—south to north, then south and west in Africa as well. In this way, settlements of these northward-moving indigenous Africans began to be established in areas along the eastern and western shores of the Nile River. Eventually, settlements of these migrating Africans reached the land areas now demarcated and known as Egypt. As these groups began inhabiting Egypt, they brought with them the culture and civilization that had been evolving along the Nile River for many generations. This south-to-north migratory pattern meant that Egypt was originally peopled by groups of neighboring Africans south of Egypt.

That the African country Egypt was originally peopled and controlled by migrating groups of their African forebears from the south is key because it allows us to determine who the original Egyptians were. Anthony Browder states:

> *In the earliest documents of the ancient Egyptians, their historians often recounted stories of their southern roots.*[21] P. 48

John Jackson, in *Introduction to African Civilization*, cites the record of the Edfu Text found in the Temple of Horus as proof that the ancient Egyptians traced their roots to Africans living to their south. Jackson points out:

---

[21] Browder, A. *Nile Valley contributions.*

According to this record civilization was brought from the south by a band of raiders under the leadership of King Horus. The followers of Horus were called Blacksmiths because they possessed iron implements. P. 93

Jackson further reported that these early groups had some roots in what is today called Somalia, although they probably originated in central Africa. The estimate is that these migrations from the south began long before 5,000 b.c. Dr. Yosef Ben-Jochannan is commonly cited for weighing in on the southern origins of the Egyptians, and quotes from the Papyrus of Hunefer: *"We came from the beginning of the Nile where the God Hapi dwells at the foothills of the Mountains of the Moon."* Browder amplifies this point by reminding that in the ki-Swahili language, Kilimanjaro means "mountains of the moon" as does the Buganda word Rwenzori, a mountain range in Democratic Republic of the Congo near the Ugandan border. It would be fair to speculate, according to Browder, that this entire region where the White Nile originates was known by the ancient Africans as the Mountains of the Moon.

Many scholars of ancient Egyptian history consider Egypt to be an extension of the civilization of Ethiopia (land of "burnt faces"), referred to as Nubia in ancient history records. W.E.B. DuBois asserts that:

By tradition, they (Egyptians) believed themselves descended not from Whites or Yellows, but from the Black peoples of the South. [22] P. 106

Kemet (Egypt) means "Black." Historical investigation, untainted by the fabrications of the Aryan model, reveals Egyptian civilization was a product of streams of indigenous Africans migrating northward along the Nile River. The

---

[22] DuBois, W. E. B., 1965 reprint. *The world and Africa.*

ancient Egyptians not only boldly proclaimed their southern roots, but also made clear that they were a Black people. The name Egypt is the Greek designation for that nation. The ancient Egyptians, however, called their nation Kemet, which means "coal black." It was represented in hieroglyphics by a block of wood burnt black at the end. The people of Kemet called themselves *Kemmiu* which means *the Blacks*. Chancellor Williams discusses how the Egyptians identified themselves:

> *There was no Egypt before the black king from whose name it was directly derived; before that the country was called Chem (Kem or Chemi [Khemi]), another name indicating its black inhabitants, and not the color of the soil, as some writers have needlessly strained themselves in asserting.* [23] P. 68

In the process of self-identification, the Egyptians of antiquity described their roots as southern and their skin as Black, but who were these Egyptians to others who lived during the age of the pharaohs? The ancient Greeks, besides spending much time in Egypt studying in the Mystery System (ancient center of learning and culture—more later), also wrote extensively about the Egyptians. H.G. Wells, in looking at the race of the ancient Egyptians, refers to the writings of the Greek fifth century b.c. historian Herodotus,

> *There can be no doubt Herodotus said that the Colchians are an Egyptian race. Before I heard any mention of the fact from others, I had remarked it myself. My own conjectures were founded, first, on the fact that they are black skinned and have wooly hair. (cited in Jackson, p. 65).* [24]

---

[23] Williams, C. 1974. *The destruction of Black civilization*.
[24] Jackson, J. 1970. *Introduction to African civilization*.

The ancient Greek Herodotus's descriptions of the people of Egypt are clear that they were Black and refined. Jackson also gives us words from the ancient Greek writer Homer, who called the Egyptians the "favorites of the Gods" and "the leading race of the world." When the Greeks spoke of the Ethiopians, the word was not referring to the country in Africa which is today called by that name. The Greeks used the term as a physical description of a people that dominated civilization in ancient times. The word "Ethiopia" comes from the Greek words *ethios* (burnt) and *ops* (face). Burnt face, for the Greeks, referred to all the lands dominated by Black people, which included all of Africa and much of western Asia.

The southern origin of Egyptian civilization cannot be underestimated in terms of its impact on history. It is key to authenticating the Blackness of the first advanced civilizations. As we look at the early Nile Valley, pay attention to the location of Nubia, the cultural predecessors of Kemet.

What do we mean by "civilization" as we explore its beginning? Neither modern dictionaries nor historians offer a definitive answer to "What is civilization?" All efforts to define it leave room for bias by one group towards others. It has been described in many ways, starting with "an advanced human society." Civilization has been described as human groups that have high levels of cultural and technical development. Others mention human groups that live in cities since the word civilization has its roots in the Latin words *civitas, civilis and civis* (city, civil, citizen).

Civilization is often explained in similar ways as descriptions of culture—largely characterized as patterns of human relationships and behaviors, often including the prevalence of arts and literature. Generally, there is a sense of having developed more complex societies, with features such as more intricate division of roles and responsibilities, expansion of knowledge, and evidence of greater innovation (such as advanced infrastructure, educational systems, arts, sciences and religion).

In western thought, it was believed that human societies advance through several stages from savagery to barbarism then finally to civilization; these views proved flawed because they are subjective and reflected high levels of ethnocentrism or superiority among those making such definitions. South African Bushmen, with their communal, peaceful culture of sharing, caring and cooperative hunting and gathering would be called barbaric using western standards, even though (unlike the Bushmen) western nations engage in the most violence known in human civilization!

Disregarding those definitions, others view common features of civilization as stable communities of people who work together and embody a moral code that respects human rights (without a focus on physical structures). One of our scholars, John G. Jackson, devoted a book chapter attempting to define civilization. He points out that while there are volumes written about civilization, few of the scholars ever tell what they mean when using the word. He acknowledges the lack of clarity as well. He does say that civilization is a form of culture and goes on to share what is meant by culture, as *"the organized behavior which the individual person learns either through training or by imitation from other members of his or her social group."*[25] Jackson concludes generally that a society can only be called civilized if it has scholars and scientists, which assumes the existence of a system of writing. Importantly he says civilizations must show progress by steadily increasing knowledge. Otherwise, the society regresses and cannot call

---

[25] Jackson, J.G. 1972. *Man, God and civilization.* P. 171

itself civilized. Either way, culture is dynamic, he shares. It moves forward or backwards. Thus, because a society once proved itself civilized, does not mean it remains so without attending to advancing itself.

No definition of civilization is complete or free of the potential for bias; so, for our purposes, we are satisfied in saying culture, the established norms, and patterns for acceptable human interaction, is one primary determinant of civilization. What's clear is that the early human groups developing in east Africa were considered our first civilizations, and a look at the nature of those cultures help us appreciate that, in many ways, the ancient groups were more civil or civilized than many nations and groups today.

> **We are satisfied with saying culture, the established norms, and patterns for acceptable human interaction, is one primary determinant of civilization.**

First Civilization Came from Nubia, Then Moved Northward

According to the unanimous testimony of the ancients, first the Ethiopians, and then the Egyptians, created and raised to an extraordinary stage of development all the elements of civilization while other peoples especially the Eurasians were still deep in barbarism. C. A. Diop, P. 230

Each civilization throughout the course of human history was built upon the accumulated knowledge and wisdom of those civilizations that preceded it. White western historians have put forth the erroneous notion that whatever little civilization African people acquired was due to their contact with the more advanced European cultures and civilizations to their north. On the contrary: All credible historical sources point to the earliest European civilizations' arrival by way of Africa, specifically the Nile Valley. Ancient civilization was emerging in central east Africa for thousands of years and spreading northward with the flow of the Nile River before Europe's first civilization (Greece) around the sixth or fifth century b.c.

The wisdom and advanced knowledge of the Nubians (located in today's northern Sudan and southern Egypt) became the ideological foundation of the Kemetic (Egyptian) civilization. Kemet ("land of the Blacks") was the offspring of the "burnt face" Nubians. The original Egyptians were migrants from Nubia. At various times during Kemet's history, pharaohs or their wives were of Nubian heritage, particularly when the two nations rivaled each other and at times one overtook the other.

Further verification of the southern roots of Egyptian culture comes from 20th Century archaeological revelations made in the southern part of Egypt near today's Lake Nasser. Bruce Williams, a University of Chicago professor and member of its Oriental Institute, analyzed artifacts unearthed in 1964 in Nubian Egypt. These provided evidence that Nubia was the foundation of knowledge upon which ancient Egyptian society was built. He published his findings in several books, sharing his research on the existence of the Black Nubian civilization, from

Ancient civilization was emerging in central east Africa for thousands of years and spreading northward with the flow of the Nile River before Europe was even born.

which Egypt's was developed. A *New York Times* science journalist wrote in 1979 about these artifacts and Dr. Williams' conclusions and begins by saying:

Evidence of the oldest recognizable monarchy in human history, preceding the rise of the earliest Egyptian kings by several generations, has been discovered in artifacts from ancient Nubia. B. Rensberger, 1979

Ancient Nubian Artifacts Yield Evidence of Earliest Monarchy

By BOYCE RENSBERGER

Evidence of the oldest recognizable monarchy in human history, preceding the rise of the earliest Egyptian kings by several generations, has been discovered in artifacts from ancient Nubia in Africa.

Until now it had been assumed that at that time the ancient Nubian culture, which existed in what is now northern Sudan and southern Egypt, had not advanced beyond a collection of scattered tribal clans and chiefdoms.

The existence of rule by kings indicates a more advanced form of political organization in which many chiefdoms are united under a more powerful and wealthier ruler.

The discovery is expected to stimulate a new appraisal of the origins of civilization in Africa, raising the question of to what extent later Egyptian culture may have derived its advanced political structure from the Nubians. The various symbols of Nubian royalty that have been found are the same as those associated, in later times, with Egyptian kings.

The new findings suggest that the ancient Nubians may have reached this stage of political development as long ago as 3300 B.C., several generations before the earliest documented Egyptian king.

The discovery is based on study of artifacts from ancient tombs excavated 15 years ago in an international effort

Continued on Page A16, Column 3

The New York Times
Published: March 1, 1979
Copyright © The New York Times

Further, the same journalist Rensberger, in 1995 shares about the greatness of ancient Nubia, including its building projects, complex government system, agricultural processes, religious systems, manufacturing and more.[26]

More than 5,000 years ago, black-skinned Africans began to create one of the most technologically and cultural sophisticated cultures that the ancient world had ever seen. It is known today as Nubia.

Location of Nubian Civilization

(prepared by Dr. Bruce Williams and the Oriental Institute)

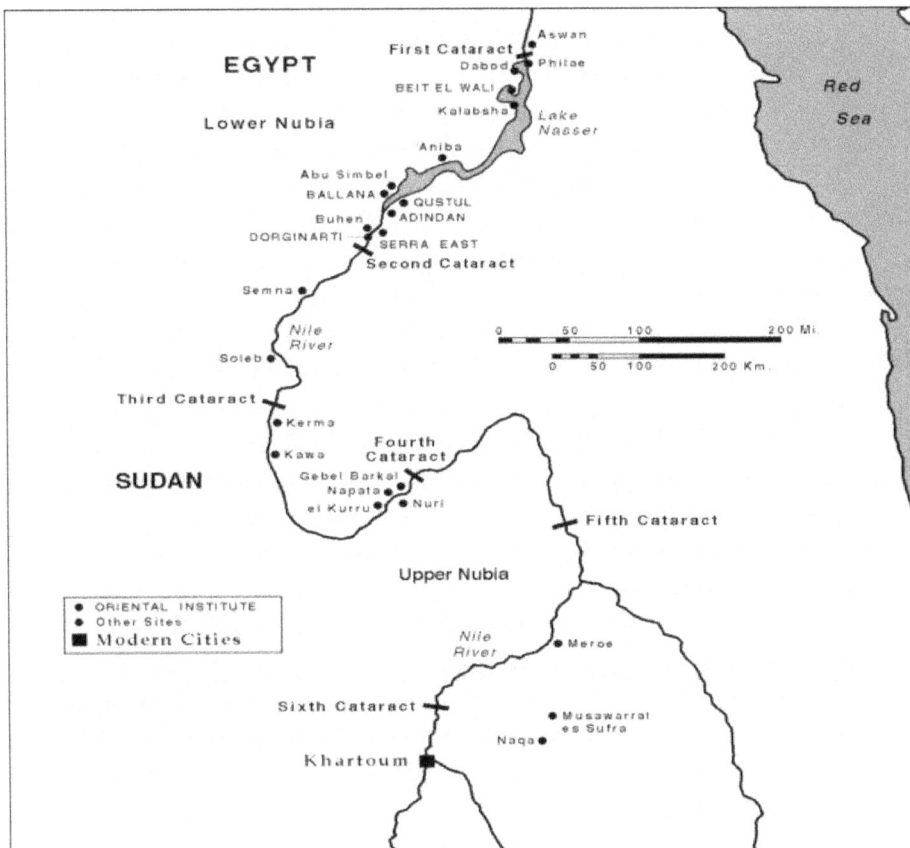

---

[26] *Washington Post.* May 10, 1995. The grandeur that was Nubia.

The earliest period of Nubian (referred to as Kush and Ta-Seti at different times) civilization is believed to have begun as early as 4,000 b.c. **_more than 1,000 years before the first Pharaonic dynasty of Egypt._** Nubia (Ta-Seti) was an expansive kingdom that stretched from the sixth cataract in Khartoum to the first cataract (during the time Nubians dominated Egypt).

Note: Cataracts are fierce rapids formed by large rocks in several places along the Nile River, between Khartoum and Aswan. There are six cataracts along the Nile River.

Analysis of the 1964 artifacts reveals that Nubian culture included religious systems and pharaohs that predated that of Egypt. Professor Bruce Williams concluded, and has been referenced by many:

> *The idea of a pharaoh may have come down the Nile from Nubia to Egypt and that would make Nubian civilization the ancestor of Egypt, at least in one critical aspect.*[27] (the designation of the leader as a "pharaoh")

The civilization of Nubia is believed to have been so advanced in these remote times that city life, architecture, and infrastructure were compared to Egypt's. Accounts speak of their agricultural wealth, their other sources of wealth and power, including as middlemen for trading between the south and north. Reported in 1992, *"Nubians were interacting with the Mediterranean world. They were literate, urbanized. They had sumptuous tombs and temples."*[28] Uncovering the full extent of Nubian civilization and comparing it to that of Kemet (Egypt) may not ever be possible because key Nubian

---

[27] Williams, C. cited in Browder, p. 55
[28] McCann, Herbert. March 22, 1992. Story of Nubia, important ancient African civilization given new life. *LA Times.*

archaeological sites now sit under several hundred feet of the waters of Lake Nasser, a man-made reservoir created by the Aswan Dam.

In summary, the advanced civilization of Kemet is an extension and expansion of Nubia. The Nile Valley cultures overlapped and were closely linked. To view Kemetic civilization in isolation from Nubia gives a flawed historical picture. This "Egypt in isolation from Africa" is *revisionist* history, and the basis for the subsequent Europeanization or Asianization of Egypt in textbooks, even to this day. In far too many history and geography texts, Kemet is classified with the "Middle East" rather than Africa. Modern depictions of ancient Egyptians tend to have European features, such as the queens Hatshepsut and Nefertiti; there's little probability that they looked anything close to white!

Section 5: IN ACTION

1. The effort to de-Blacken Egypt was another way of reinforcing negative stereotypes about Blackness. What are some of the myths about "blackness" you hear in your environment?

   _____

   _____

   _____

   _____

2. Conduct an internet search on *"Black racial stereotypes"* and discuss with your group what you found and the possible modern-day causes of it.

3. The facts of the matter. Review the following questions posed at the beginning of the chapter. What do you know now that you did not know before?

   a. Why and when did it become important for European historians to de-Africanize Egypt?_____

   b. The Nile River flows through several African countries enabling ancient civilizations to flourish. Name five of those countries.

      _____

   c. There were African civilizations older than Egypt. What is one new thing you learned about this idea?

      _____

Section **6**

AFRICA

Egypt & Contributions to World Civilization

Mate Masie
Knowledge, wisdom

Highlights:

1. Egypt's advanced civilization, appropriated by European historians
2. A general timeline of Egyptian civilization

Words Worth Heeding: "*That the ancient Egyptians were African is a belief which was not denied in Europe until about 1830. The Greeks had made this clear and they had also emphasized the primacy of Egyptian civilization…The shift in the intellectual climate belongs to the rise of modern European imperialism.*" -Ivan Van Sertima

Much research has been devoted to ancient Egypt, the land of the Blacks. Evidence shows the highest level of ancient civilization was in Africa.

Check out your mind

1. There were many great pharaohs in Egypt. Name two that helped build the great monuments.

   _____   _____

2. What are two significant Nile Valley/Egyptian *firsts* that contributed to world civilization?

   _____

3. Name two things Europeans came to Egypt to learn that they could not learn in their own land.

   _____

   _____

At a time between the seventh and sixth centuries b.c. Greeks began migrating to the Nile Valley in search for enlightenment in every facet of human endeavor. Ancient Egypt was well-developed in areas such as academics, governance, religion and culture. This is especially glaring when juxtaposed with their late-arriving northern

Greek neighbors. Nothing in the European world at that time was comparable to the high achievement of ancient Egypt. Exposure to the learning centers of Africa, a few thousand years after Egypt built great civilizations, provided the basis for the widely acclaimed ideas of famed Greek philosophers and mathematicians, including Socrates, Plato, Thales, Pythagoras, and others. In truth, Greece was an offshoot of the Nile Valley, not the originators of civilization as asserted by modern European historians. White historians trace the current knowledge of science, ideas about democracy, and the existential purpose of humanity back to Greek writers. What they are psychologically unable or unwilling to acknowledge is that if western culture and civilization are products of ancient Greece, then they are indebted to the Africans of the Nile Valley who educated the Greeks.

Egypt's Advanced Civilization, Appropriated by Europeans

What follows merely skims the surface of ancient Egypt's contributions to world civilization. Esteemed Black academics have written volumes about ancient Egypt. For a more thorough examination, George James, Dr. Yosef Ben-Jochannan, Ivan Van Sertima, John G. Jackson and W.E.B. Dubois provide rich and thorough treatises on Africa's first civilizations, especially Egypt. Why so much about Egypt? Put simply, there's far more available Egyptian writing and artifacts to allow the unraveling of this region's history than there are remains of any of the other Nile Valley civilizations.

Three areas of ancient Egypt's high achievement, but by no means the only areas, are: *religion/spirituality, architectural projects, and advanced learning centers*. The achievements in just these three broad areas have implications for the high level of human development and civilization during ancient times, some of which are still unrivaled.

The Quest for Spiritual Consciousness 5,000 Years Ago. Studying Egyptian and other Nile Valley cultures reveals a continuing effort to comprehend the mysteries of the universe. In an ongoing pursuit to improve the quality of human life, these east Africans believed it necessary to understand the mysterious celestial bodies and cosmic forces that created, organized and sustained everything existing in the universe. In the Nile Valley, at least 2,000 years before the emergence of Christianity, all of life was viewed as religious activity carried out within the context of those celestial bodies and cosmic forces. The Nile Valley dwellers focused their lives around exploring and conforming to the spiritual realities which were at the core of all knowledge and existence.

Responding to this spiritual quest took two forms:

1) The development of a set of moral-ethical principles that reflected the order and organization of the universe
2) The construction of buildings that could function as centers for studying, meditating, and exploring the spiritual realms of existence

The Egypt/Nile Valley development of theological, moral and ethical principles, the foundation of the world's major religions, flourished during the Golden Age of Kemet—the Third through Sixth Dynasties of the Old Kingdom (2650-2150 B.C.). Conquerors from Nubia traveled northward into Kemet and established the Third Dynasty[29]. They were primarily responsible for the ideological and cultural fruits of the Golden Age.

---

[29]Jackson, J. 1970. *Introduction to African civilization.*

Major Pharaoh's of the Golden Age—Age of the Pyramids
(Kemet's 3rd through 6th Dynasties)

Note: All dates are estimates, with different sources offering slight differences

- **KING ZOSER (2667-2648 b.c.);** 2nd king of the Third Dynasty; the builder of the first pyramid, the *Step Pyramid* and Saqqara complex, designed by Imhotep

- **KING KHUFU KHEOPS (2589 – 2566 b.c.);** 2nd king of the 4th Dynasty; builder of the *Great Pyramid at Giza*, based on Imhotep's design 100+ years earlier.

- **KING KHAFRE (2558-2532 b.c.);** 4th king of the 4th Dynasty; builder of the *Sphinx at Giza*.

- **KING UNAS (2375-2345 b.c.);** 8th and final king of the Fifth Dynasty, ruled 15-30 years; *Pyramid Texts* were inscribed in his tomb.

- **KING TETI (2345-2333 b.c.);** 1st king of the Sixth Dynasty and **KING PEPI** (2289-2255); 3rd king of the Sixth Dynasty; *Pyramid Texts* inscribed in their tombs.

Beginning of Monotheism. Speaking generally, the theological views of the Nile Valley as recorded and practiced in Kemet, held that there was one supreme power (God) or a being that is the center of creation and existed within everything throughout the universe (i.e., monotheism, one God). Each aspect of the One supreme, transcendent power was called *Netcherw* (plural) or *Netcher* (singular). The Netcherw were not God as supreme being but represented specific aspects and manifestations of that ultimate power.

Each Netcher was associated with an animal that reflected its unique spiritual principle or role. Of these, a few were:

- ***Netcher Heru (Horus)*** was depicted as a man with the head of a falcon usually with its right eye displayed. The falcon's right eye symbolized spiritual awareness and enlightenment; the capacity to perceive the inner reality of beings.

- ***Netcher Djhuiti*** was depicted as a man with the head of Ibis, a bird that assumes the shape of a heart when it sleeps. In Kemet, the heart is the location of the soul. The Ibis's head is often turned so that its left eye is displayed. The Netcher Djhuiti is the Keeper of the Secrets of Science and Healing. (The Greek name for Djhuiti is Thoth). In the Greek pantheon of Gods, Thoth became Hermes.

- ***Netcher Set*** was depicted as a man with the head of an ass. It symbolized the recalcitrant or rebellious nature of the human spirit.

These Netcherw along with others were not a reflection of polytheistic religion in Kemet[30], but a recognition of the omnipotence of the one transcendent, supreme being (God) having many different manifestations. The inhabitants of the Nile Valley discovered thousands of years ago that there was no structure, function, process, or life form which was not a part of and embodied by that One supreme power.

The oldest written record of the theology of Kemet and the Nile Valley cultures is contained in the Pyramid Texts. These writings were found in the pyramids of the Pharaohs Unas (8th and final king of the 2375-2345 b.c. Fifth Dynasty) and Teti and

---

[30] Browder, A.

Pepi (both of the Sixth Dynasty from 2345-2255 b.c.). Dr. Maulana Karenga[31] calls the Pyramid Texts the oldest existing religious writings. These writings were placed in the pyramids of these pharaohs over 4,000 years ago.

One important set of writings in these texts was the *Declaration of Virtues*. These writings delineate the moral claims one must be able to make to attain salvation. Another set of significant writings in the Pyramid Texts (inscribed on the walls of the pyramids at least 2,500 years b.c.) was the Sebait or *Book of Wise Instruction*, which offered wise sayings, instructions for living—in other words, general

The Pyramid Texts are the oldest existing religious writings. These writings were placed in the pyramids of these pharaohs over 4,000 years ago.

principles by which to live one's life. (The biblical *Book of Wisdom* does something similar and was written much later, around 200 b.c.). The oldest *Book of Wise Instruction* is the book *The Teachings of Ptahotep*. This *oldest book in the world* dealt with the important concept of *Maat*, a system of morals and ethics, which was central to the religious life of Kemet. *Maat* defines the basis of righteousness and a life worthy of salvation. According to Ptahotep,

> *If you are a man who leads, a man who controls the affairs of many, then seek the most perfect way of performing your responsibility so that your conduct is blameless. Great is Maat (truth, justice, and righteousness). It is everlasting.*

---

[31] Karenga, M. 1989. *Selections from the Husia—Sacred wisdom of ancient Egypt.*

Maat has been unchanged since the time of Ausar. Baseness may obtain riches,

yet crime lands its wares on the shore. In the end, only Maat lasts. [32]

The theology, moral teachings, rituals, and mythology of ancient Kemet influenced the beliefs and practices of all the world's major religions including Judaism and Christianity. The central moral teachings of Judaism are the Ten Commandments which Moses received from God at Mount Sinai. Over 1,000 years before Moses received those commandments, the **42 Admonitions of Maat** were placed in the tombs of pharaohs of the fifth and sixth dynasties.

When these two writings are compared, as follows, the similarities are striking. The Ten Commandments are clearly a modification and abridged version of the **42 Admonitions of Maat** (also called **42 Negative Confessions** or **Declaration of Innocence**). The relationship between the two moral teachings is easy to understand when we recall that according to the Bible record Moses (rescued from the Nile River) grew up and was educated in Kemet (Egypt) among the royal family at some time during the 13th Century b.c.

> **Note:** In reviewing the following version of **The 42 Admonitions of Maat**, know that there are a number of translations of this ancient text. All are very similar, and some include lengthier entries. This version is shared widely and includes duplications in #20 and #21. One of the other versions of #21 states "I have not been angry without reason."

---

[32] Morentz, S. 1960 and 1973. *Egyptian religion.*, translated by Ann E. Keep, p. 115

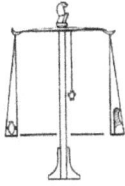

The Netcher Maat was associated with the seven cardinal virtues, the keys to human perfectibility: truth, justice, propriety, harmony, balance, reciprocity and order. The seven virtues and the 42 Admonitions of Maat were the guidelines for correct moral behavior. They were written approximately 1,500 years before the Ten Commandments.

The 42 Admonitions of Maat

1. I have not done iniquity.
2. I have not robbed with violence.
3. I have not stolen.
4. I have done no murder; I have done no harm.
5. I have not defrauded offerings.
6. I have not diminished obligations.
7. I have not plundered the Netcher.
8. I have not spoken lies.
9. I have not snatched away food.
10. I have not caused pain.
11. I have not committed fornication.
12. I have not caused shedding of tears.
13. I have not dealt deceitfully.
14. I have not transgressed.
15. I have not acted guilefully.
16. I have not laid waste the ploughed land.
17. I have not been an eavesdropper.
18. I have not set my lips in motion (against any man).
19. I have not been angry and wrathful except for a just cause.
20. I have not defiled the wife of any man.
21. I have not defiled the wife of any man.
22. I have not polluted myself.
23. I have not caused terror.
24. I have not transgressed.
25. I have not burned with rage.
26. I have not stopped my ears against the words of Right and Truth (Maat).
27. I have not worked grief.
28. I have not acted with insolence.
29. I have not stirred up strife.
30. I have not judged hastily.
31. I have not been an eavesdropper.
32. I have not multiplied words exceedingly.
33. I have not done neither harm nor ill.
34. I have never cursed the king.
35. I have never fouled the water.
36. I have not spoken scornfully.
37. I have never cursed the Netcher.
38. I have not stolen.
39. I have not defrauded the offerings of the Netcherw.
40. I have not plundered the offerings to the blessed dead.
41. I have not filched the food of the infant, neither have I sinned against the Netcher of my native town.
42. I have not slaughtered with evil intent the cattle of the Netcher.

Ten Commandments

(The Commandments which are similar to the 42 Declarations are highlighted by parenthesis)

1. I am the Lord thy God. Thou shalt have no other gods before me. (41)
2. Thou shalt not make unto thee any graven image...
3. Thou shalt not take the name of the Lord thy God in vain... (7, 37, 41)
4. Remember the Sabbath day, to keep it holy...
5. Honor thy father and mother. (1, 12, 28)
6. Thou shalt not kill. (4)
7. Thou shalt not commit adultery. (11, 20, 21)
8. Thou shalt not steal. (2, 3, 5, 6, 7, 9, 39, 40)
9. Though shalt not bear false witness against thy neighbor. (8, 13, 18, 29)
10. Thou shalt not covet thy neighbor's house or wife... (13, 20, 21, 29, 33)

Nile Valley Contributions To Civilization / Study Guide

22

33

---

[33] Browder, A. 1994. *Nile Valley contributions to civilization, study guide.* p. 22

Also, Akhenaton's *Hymn to Aton* (written during the New Kingdom around 1353 b.c.) is remarkably similar to *Psalm 104*, thought to have been written by King David around 1000 b.c.

One Comparison of Egypt Religious Thought & the Bible

Akhenaton's Hymn (ca. 1353 b.c.)	Psalms 104 (ca. 1000 b.c.)
The world is in darkness like the dead. Every lion cometh forth from its den; all serpents sting. Darkness reigns.	Thou makest the darkness and it is night, wherein all the beasts of the forest do creep forth. They young lions roar after their prey…
When Thou risest in the horizon…the darkness is banished…Then in all the world they do their work.	The sun riseth…Man goeth forth unto his work and to his labor until the evening.
All trees and plants flourish…the birds flutter in their marshes…All sheep dance upon their feet.	The trees of the Lord are full of sap…wherein the birds their nests…The high hills are a refuge for the wild goats.
The ships sail upstream and downstream alike…The fish in the river leap up before thee; and thy rays are in the midst of the great sea.	So is this great and wide sea, wherein are things creeping innumerable, both small and great and beasts…There go the ships.
How manifold are all Thy works?…Thou didst create the earth according to Thy desire, mean all cattle…all that are upon the earth.	O Lord how manifold are thy works? In wisdom has Thou made them all…The earth is full of thy creatures.

The Holy Trinity, at the center of Christian theology and faith was preceded by a Holy Trinity in Nubia (3300 b.c.) and later in Kemet 2,000 years before the birth of Jesus. The legend of Ausar (Osiris), Auset (Isis), and Heru (Horus) parallels the legends of the birth, death and resurrection of Jesus.[34]

---

34 Ben-Jochannan, Y., Finch, C., Oduyoye, M. 1987. *The Afrikan origins of the major world religions*

The story, in brief, unfolds in this way:

Ausar (Osiris) and Auset (Isis) were married. Ausar was slain by his evil brother Set (similar to the Bible's Cain who murders his brother Abel). Set cuts his brother's body into 14 pieces and spreads them all over Kemet. Auset finds all the pieces of her husband's body except the phallus (penis), which according to the story was swallowed by a fish. Auset then recreates the missing part in the form of an obelisk (which in Kemet became a symbol of resurrection or restoration). The Netcher Djhuiti gives Auset divine words to resurrect Ausar. Before Ausar was resurrected Auset was divinely impregnated and immaculately conceived her son Heru (Horus). When Heru became an adult, he avenged his father's murder by killing his uncle Set. Heru then reigned as king on earth. Ausar, referred to as the good shepherd, ruled the underworld and presided over the final judgement of the deceased.

Heru, as king on earth, is symbolized by the sun disk and the head of a falcon. Heru is the "light of the world" and in slaying his uncle Set represents the triumph of good over evil, or the light of righteousness over darkness. In the *Kemetic Holy Trinity* all the key symbols associated with the much-later Christian Trinity story are present:

1. An annunciation and virgin birth
2. A crucifixion or murder of the righteous by the unrighteous
3. Resurrection
4. A perpetual reign of the righteous and the resurrected over the kingdoms of life and death

There have been more than 200 parallels noted between the biblical stories of Jesus and the Nile Valley religious writings about Osiris and Horus.[35] These striking similarities between the stories, symbols, and writings of the Nile Valley cultures and the religions of Judaism and Christianity point to the African origin of the major religions. All the world's major religions are built upon the theological principles, morals, rituals, and myths that originated in Nile Valley cultures. The same kind of comparison of religious belief, ritual and mythology was made by Godfrey

> **There have been more than 200 parallels noted between the biblical stories of Jesus and the Nile Valley religious writings about Osiris and Horus.**

Higgins in his book *Anacalypsis*[36] over 100 years ago; he discovered the same African roots existed in Hinduism and Buddhism, which are older than Christianity. He shows similarities in numerous areas including the Trinity, crucifixion and ascension of the Savior.

The Great Building Projects. During the Golden Age of the Old Kingdom, an impressive amount of construction took place. The greatest and most complex structures ever built in the world were erected during the Old Kingdom, which was known as the Pyramid Age demonstrating the math and science prowess of our forebears. During his reign, **Pharaoh Djoser (Zoser)** had the **Step Pyramid** built and a vast temple complex at Saqqara, near Cairo, Egypt. Anthony Browder, in *Nile Valley Contributions to Civilization,* describes the Step Pyramid as the **world's first**

---

[35] Gerald Massey (Ancient Egypt, the light of the world), cited by Browder, Nile Valley Contributions to Civilization.
[36] Higgins, G. 1836. *Anacalypsis, attempt to draw aside the veil of Saitic Isis…*

skyscraper. The **Step Pyramid** was 197 feet tall. What are the implications of that during these ancient times? For one, we can be assured that there were great architects of African descent during these ancient times. For this pyramid, its chief architect was Imhotep, one of the most brilliant and multi-skilled men that ever lived. Besides being an architect, Imhotep was an astronomer, philosopher and physician. The Saqqara complex was made up of 15 pyramids along with several temples.

A few miles northeast of Cairo is where the **Great Pyramid** was constructed approximately 50 years after the Step Pyramid. Built during the Fourth Dynasty under **Pharaoh Khufu**, the Great Pyramid is 481 feet tall (more than twice as high as the Step Pyramid) and contains over 1.3 million stone blocks, each with an average weight of 2.5 tons. It is one of today's seven wonders of the world and is one of the three major pyramids in the Giza complex. The others are the Pyramid of Khafre and Pyramid of Menkaure. According to Browder, what is especially astounding about

What is not commonly recognized is that there were more than 70 pyramids built by the inhabitants of the Nile Valley.

the construction of the pyramids, besides their sheer size, is the astronomical orientation and mathematical relationships of these structures. Says Browder:

> *The fact that the Great Pyramid was engineered with accuracies measured to the hundredths of an inch, is a testimonial to its builders having possessed an advanced knowledge of mathematics.* P. 106

What is not commonly recognized is that there were more than 70 pyramids built by the inhabitants of the Nile Valley. Besides the Saqqara's 15, other pyramids have been discovered along the Nile in Nubia and Kush (a province within ancient Nubia).

There are almost twice as many pyramids in the Sudan than in Egypt. These are noted as not as tall as the major ones in Egypt, and they were believed built later. Most of these are situated between the 3rd and 4th cataract. [37]Similar architectural expertise is displayed when considering the construction of pyramids outside of Africa, particularly in Peru, Mexico, and Guatemala.

The Great Pyramid of the Giza Complex

---

[37] Castellano, N. March 17, 2020. The Nubian kingdom of Kush, rival to Egypt. *National Geographic.*

The amazing Sphinx. In addition to the pyramids, there is another spectacular structure that reflects the architectural and engineering brilliance of the ancient inhabitants of the Nile Valley. This is the Great Sphinx, located at Giza in front of the Great Pyramid and built between the Third and Fourth Dynasties (around 2558-2532 during the reign of Pharaoh Khafre, the builder of the second pyramid of Giza)[38]. What is so remarkable about the Great Sphinx is that it was carved out of one massive stone. *"It is the largest and oldest monument ever sculpted from a single rock"* (Browder). The Sphinx faces east towards the rising sun and **is at the foot of the Great Pyramid.** It is 240 feet long and 66.3 feet high. It is comprised of the body of a lion and the head of a man.

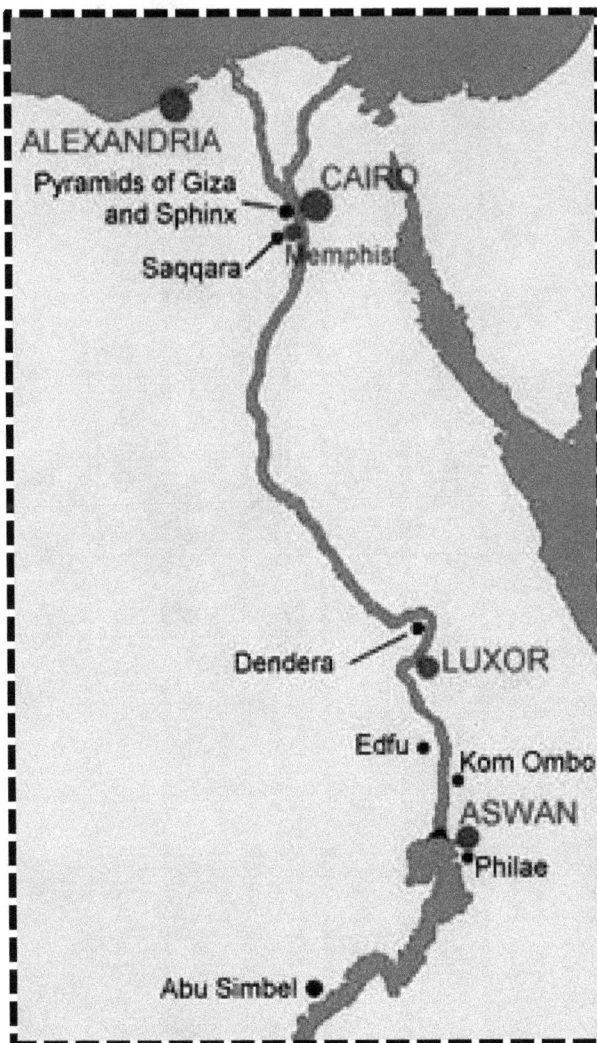

Location of Saqqara in Egypt

As with all the great physical structures in the Nile Valley, the Great Sphinx had deep spiritual significance. It was originally called Her-Em-Aket (Heru of the Horizon). This associated the monument with the Netcher God of the sun or spiritual light Heru. The blending of an animal's body with the head of a

---

[38] Van Sertima, I. 1993. *Egypt revisited.*

man symbolizes the dual nature of humanity—divine and human. The Great Sphinx sitting at the foot of the Great Pyramid faces the east and the rising sun in the morning and the star constellations in the evening.

Besides the **Great Sphinx** (pictured below in modern form with the "African" nose removed), there were other sphinxes in the Nile Valley. Within the city of Luxor (Waset), which took the place of Memphis as the capital of Kemet, there were two

major temples, the Luxor Temple and the Karnak Temple. There are **1,300 sphinxes** lining the road for over one mile connecting these two temples.

Many other expressions of the architectural and engineering genius of the ancient Nile Valley Africans are seen in the numerous temples they built. Their significance went well beyond being houses of worship as understood in today's world. Like the pyramids, the temples were built to conform to specific celestial bodies and the mathematics related to the movements of those bodies.

Temples were built with openings that allowed light from a specific star or star constellation to enter a specific chamber at an exact angle. The seasonal changes marked by the sun's movement between the northern and southern hemispheres was used as a blueprint to construct the orientation of a temple. This was possible because of the advanced knowledge of astronomy that the Nile Valley inhabitants had already accumulated. The day the seasons changed could be determined by measuring the condition of the light from the sun penetrating a specific area of the temple. A British astronomer, Norman Lockyer, studying the Karnak Temple, concluded it was so perfectly built in regard to the movement of the Earth, and associated with the summer solstice, that *"a beam of light coming through a narrow passage some 500 yards all the way to a properly oriented sanctuary would be there no more than a couple of minutes and then pass away."* [39]

The Mystery System for Advanced Education. The temples in ancient Kemet and the entire Nile Valley were centers for the education of great philosophers, scientists, and mathematicians. In the Nile Valley cultures, which held no separation between

---

[39] Browder, A. p. 117

the sacred and secular, every academic discipline was viewed as a pathway to gain knowledge of the Divine (God). This was not a knowing of God in a narrow, rational sense, but knowledge of God as an inner experience of self-discovery and self-realization. This earthly inner experience of and union with the Divine was the definition of salvation among the Nile Valley cultures.

The course of study for those who attended the temples was called the **Mystery System**; it brought the learner to a profound awakening to the mysterious nature of the relationship between oneself and the cosmos. This level of understanding allowed the "student" entry into a heightened level of consciousness and the experience of salvation (union with God). George James, author of *Stolen Legacy*, identified five areas that formed the curriculum of the temple and its Mystery System. They are:

Mystery System Curriculum		
	Seven liberal arts	grammar, arithmetic, rhetoric, dialectic, geometry, astronomy, and music
	Sciences/41 books of Thoth (Hermes)	hieroglyphics, cosmography, topography, physiology, diseases, embalming, anatomy, and drugs
	Sciences of the monuments	pyramids, temples, libraries, obelisks, sphinxes, and idols
	The secret sciences	numerical symbolism, geometrical symbolism, magic, the book of the dead, myths, and parables
	The social order and its protection	economics, civics, law, government, statistics, census taking, ship building, military science, the manufacture of chariots, and horse breeding

The late Dr. Yosef Ben-Jochannan identified three ascending grades or levels within this Mystery System curriculum. A student had to pass through all three levels to be ordained into the priesthood. These were:

1. **Mortals**—students on probation and under instruction who had not yet achieved experience into the inner vision

2. **Intelligences**—those students who had attained inner vision and received *mind* or "nous"

3. **Creators or Sons of Light**—those students who became a part of the spiritual consciousness

It was through rigorous study in the Mystery System that the major Greek philosophers and mathematicians gained their knowledge. Socrates, Plato, Pythagoras, Thales, Heraclitus, and others all studied in the temples of Kemet, receiving instruction about the Mystery System, which was the foundation of ancient civilization. Europe has proclaimed that the roots of its civilization harken back to the ideas of the major Greek philosophers. If that is the case, Europe owes much to the Africans who were their instructors, guides, and exemplars.

This section offered a cursory look at the architectural, intellectual, religious, scientific, and cultural advancements of ancient Kemet and the rest of the east African Nile Valley. These innovations and hallmarks of civilization were accomplished long before Africans and Europeans began to interact with each other. And those first interactions found Europeans flocking to the Nile Valley to learn from their master teachers.

General Timeline of Ancient Egypt

The Nile Valley[40]
B.C. (before the common era); a.d. (after the common era)

8000 – 5000 B.C.	Earliest Nubian societies emerge (Kemetic name for Nubia: Nubia Ta Net Jer, "God's Land")
3800	Nubia kingdom of Ta Seti ("Land of the Bow") The control of King Ta Seti extended into Upper Egypt. Ta Seti kings wore a white crown and used the symbol of the Falcon God Heru (Horus)

A dynasty was made up of the rule of a series of leaders from the same family. A new dynasty began when one family conquered another or there were no heirs to take control.

3150 – 2700 (Kemet Dynasties 1 and 2)	King Narmer (Menes) unifies Upper and Lower Kemet and locates capital at Memphis; Narmer was the first founder of Kemet.
Old Kingdom & Pyramid Age **2700-2150 (Kemet Dynasties 3-6)**	King Zoser (2667 – 2648); 2nd king of the Third Dynasty; the builder of the Step Pyramid and Saqqara complex, designed by **Imhotep**, first architect and physician King Khufu Kheops (2589-2566); 2nd king of the 4th Dynasty; builder of the Great Pyramid at Giza King Khafre (2558-2532). 4th king of the 4th Dynasty; builder of the Sphinx. King Unas (2375-2345); 8th king of the Fifth Dynasty; Pyramid Texts were inscribed in his tomb. King Teti (2345-2333); 1st king of the Sixth Dynasty and King Pepi (2289-2255); 3rd king of the Sixth Dynasty; Pyramid Texts inscribed in both of their tombs.
2140-2040 (1st First Intermediate Period/Dynasties 7-10)	

---

[40] Compiled from multiple sources.

2040 – 1640 (Middle Kingdom/Dynasties 11-13)	King Mentuhotep Nebhepetre; 1st king of the 11th Dynasty; again reunites the two kingdoms; 2nd founder of Kemet; relocates capital to Waset (Luxor or Thebes)
1640-1540 (2nd Intermediate Period/Dynasties 14-17)	First Asian invasion of Kemet by the Hyksos (rulers of foreign lands)
1540-1070 (New Kingdom/Dynasties 18-20)	King Ahmose I (1540-1501); 1st king of the 18th Dynasty; extends control of Kemet to the Euphrates River
	Hatshepsut (1473-1458); 18th Dynasty; rules Kemet as first female pharaoh.
	King Amenhotep IV (Akhenaton, 1353-1335); 10th king of the 18th Dynasty; introduces concept of Aton as one single God and rejects the notion of worshipping Netcherw. Queen Nefertiti rules with him.
	King Ramses II (1290-1224); 3rd king of the 19th Dynasty; rules during the time of Hebrew Exodus from Kemet. Some Kemetic historians believe the Exodus was of followers of Akhenaton whose religious ideas had been denounced. Queen Nefertari was his co-regent.
1070-750 (Third Intermediate Period, 21-24 Dynasties)	
750-332 (Late Kingdom) **25-31 Dynasties**	King Piye (Piankhi, 750 – 712); 2nd king of the 25th Dynasty; Nubian king gains control of Upper and Lower Kemet
	King Tanutamun (664-657); 6th king of 25th Dynasty; keeps control of Upper Egypt after Asians invade Lower Egypt.
	King Cambyses II (525-522); 1st king of 27th Dynasty and of Persian descent; Persians invade Kemet and defeat Egyptian king; capital of Kemet moved to Babylon.
	King Amyrtalos (404-399); 1st king of 28th Dynasty; expels Persians from Kemet.
	King Nectanebo (380-362); 1st king of 31st Dynasty; first Persian king after 2nd invasion of Kemet.
332-30	Alexander of Greece defeats Persian army and conquers Kemet

Greco-Roman Period

146 b.c.	Romans defeat the Greeks
30 b.c. – 323 a.d.	Rome claims Kemet as one of its provinces

The Common Era begins (a.d. or a.c.e.)

323-642 a.d.	In 323, Constantine converts to Christianity and makes it the official state religion
	In 391, the Roman Christian Emperor Theodosius bans ancient Mystery Systems of Kemet and closes all temples.
	In 642, the first invasion of Moslems in Africa takes place. Kemet is conquered and Islam is introduced to the inhabitants.

This is not a complete list of all the pharaohs of Kemet. Only those who reigned during times when events of significant importance to the history of Kemet are listed.

The designations b.c.e. and a.c.e. refer to periods before the common era and after the common era. They take the place of the Christian-centered organization of history/time (b.c. and a.d.)

Intermediate periods were times of great internal crisis and instability within Kemet. Often the unity between Upper and Lower was severed and political upheaval was rampant.

Section 6 IN ACTION

1. Name three of the most famed pharaohs and their contributions to the earliest civilizations.

   _____

   _____

   _____

2. Conduct an internet search to list as many of the "ancient Egyptian contributions to civilization." List at least five that you did not know.

   _____   _____

   _____   _____

   _____   _____

   _____   _____

3. Ancient Egypt's center of advanced learning was called:

   _____

4. Besides Egypt, what is at least one other place where Africans built pyramids?_____

5. List three stories that are similar in both Nile Valley religion and Christianity.

   _____

   _____

   _____

Section **7**

AFRICA

Other Major African Civilizations
Before the Rise of Europe

Adinkrahene (Adinkra King) Leadership, Greatness, Charisma

Highlights:

1. Golden Age of West Africa *before* the European onslaught
2. Other West African Kingdoms as Europeans arrive

Words Worth Heeding: *"Nothing in Africa had any European influence before 332 B.C. If you have 10,000 years behind you before you even saw a European, then who gave you the idea that he moved from the ice-age, came all the way into Africa and built a great civilization and disappeared, when he had not built a shoe for himself or a house with a window?"*

-Dr. John H. Clarke

Africans established advanced civilizations throughout the Continent, many renowned ones in west Africa. These were envied by Europeans during their Dark Ages.

Check out your mind

1. What are two significant west African empires/kingdoms that were a part of the Golden Age of West Africa?

   _____   _____

2. What was one key feature of Europe while west Africa was basking in its Golden Age?

   _____

3. What were two characteristics of the west African cultures' greatness?

   _____
   _____

W e turn now to a few vexing questions to be addressed in these final two sections of ***Connections Remembered***. Both the astute student of African and world history and the less informed might wonder about such questions as these: *What transpired between ancient Africa's grandeur, replete with the world's firsts, and the 21st Century reality of Black life in America and throughout the Diaspora? How is it that Black people everywhere find ourselves despised, denigrated and disregarded, so far from that* *former glory, fighting for every opportunity solely based on our skin pigmentation? Why can't we just shake off slavery's "moment in time" and recapture our glory?*

These next pages serve as a bridge from our ancient, glorious "then" to now. These latter sections, we hope, reconnect us to the chain of memories of the era of west African glory and how it was abruptly disrupted by devastating, genocidal experiences that make reclaiming Black healthy identity still a challenge today. While volumes can be and have been written about the intervening millennia and centuries from the ancient civilizations to 400 years of oppression, the records remain scant and imprecise. Be reminded that much of Africa's history of accomplishment has been either 1) destroyed by the conquering European oppressors or 2) poorly documented. ***The effort to "erase" our past is part of the systematic strategy to make of Black people permanent slaves—kept in place through the relentless effort to create in us an enduring "psychological" bondage that requires no physical bonds.***

Great West African Cultures *Before* the European Onslaught

Culture and civilization not only flowed north, but also south, west, and east out from Africa's human birthplace—the Nile Valley. West Africa was *one* beneficiary of those Nile Valley hallmarks, which demarcated the signs of civilization from barbarism. A cursory examination of West Africa's history demonstrates many nations there evolved and expanded their social, cultural, intellectual, political, and religious systems to new and distinctive heights. When we explore these cultures, it is clear they demonstrate that many west African nations were both borrowers from the early inventiveness of Nile Valley Africans and innovators in their own right.

We've "Known Ancient Dusty Rivers". These advanced civilizations and refined social systems germinated along many of Africa's waterways. Following the paths of some of the most prolific rivers and lakes in the world, Africans birthed renowned cultures along not only the Nile and the African Great Lakes in the east, but also along West Africa's **Lake Chad, River Senegal, River Gambia, River Niger, Volta River** (among others) and southern Africa's **Zambezi River**. As 1920's poet Langston Hughes reminded us: we've *"known rivers ancient as the world and older than the flow of human blood in human veins."*

West Africa's history provides a critical link to understanding both our grandeur and our suffering, as it was both the setting of one of the most glorious ages in world civilization and subsequently the most horrendous human bondage and anguish.

Every generation of Black young people must know about and connect to the greatness of western Africa for several reasons. West Africa's history provides a critical link to understanding both our grandeur and our suffering, as it was both the setting of one of the most glorious ages in world civilization and subsequently the most horrendous human bondage and anguish. Every Black child should know their roots are likely there. Yes, the ancestral roots of Blacks in North America and the Caribbean are planted along West African shores and the western interior. These lands were where our ancestors spawned what is referred to as **The Golden Age of West Africa**. This glimpse of West Africa's ancient history provides some context for understanding the last 400+ years of Black oppression and subjugation—with vestiges that continue to have bearing on the Black experience in America and throughout the Diaspora.

Indebted to our Scholars. We have been bequeathed a trove of rigorous research to borrow from, share and build upon. Several of our now-deceased preeminent scholars devoted their lives to uncovering and documenting the advanced culture and civilizations of Black Africa, long before the arrival of the Europeans. These luminaries, whose works should *always* have a place on our bookshelves, include:

- Dr. Josef Ben-Jochannan, *Black Man of the Nile* and *African Origins of the Major Western Religions*

- Lerone Bennett, *Before the Mayflower*

- Dr. Cheikh Anta Diop, *The African Origin of Civilization: Myth or Reality*

- John Hope Franklin, *From Slavery to Freedom*

- John G. Jackson, *Introduction to African Civilization*

- George James, *Stolen Legacy*

- Dr. Ivan Van Sertima, *They Came Before Columbus* and *The Golden Age of the Moor'*

- Chancellor Williams, *The Destruction of Black Civilization*

Their published, oft-cited works delved into not only the earliest civilizations in the world along the Nile, they also used their genius to uncover and amplify the stories of African cultures that spread into West Africa, South Africa, and likely the whole of Black Africa, and the Americas *before* the rise of Europe. Their treatises meticulously debunk the fabricated Europe-centered view of world history.

Civilization Spreads Across Africa. Black African cultures spanned much of the area now known as the Sahara Desert. **The Sahara was not always a desert**; it was a place of flourishing cultures. Civilization spread west from the Nile Valley

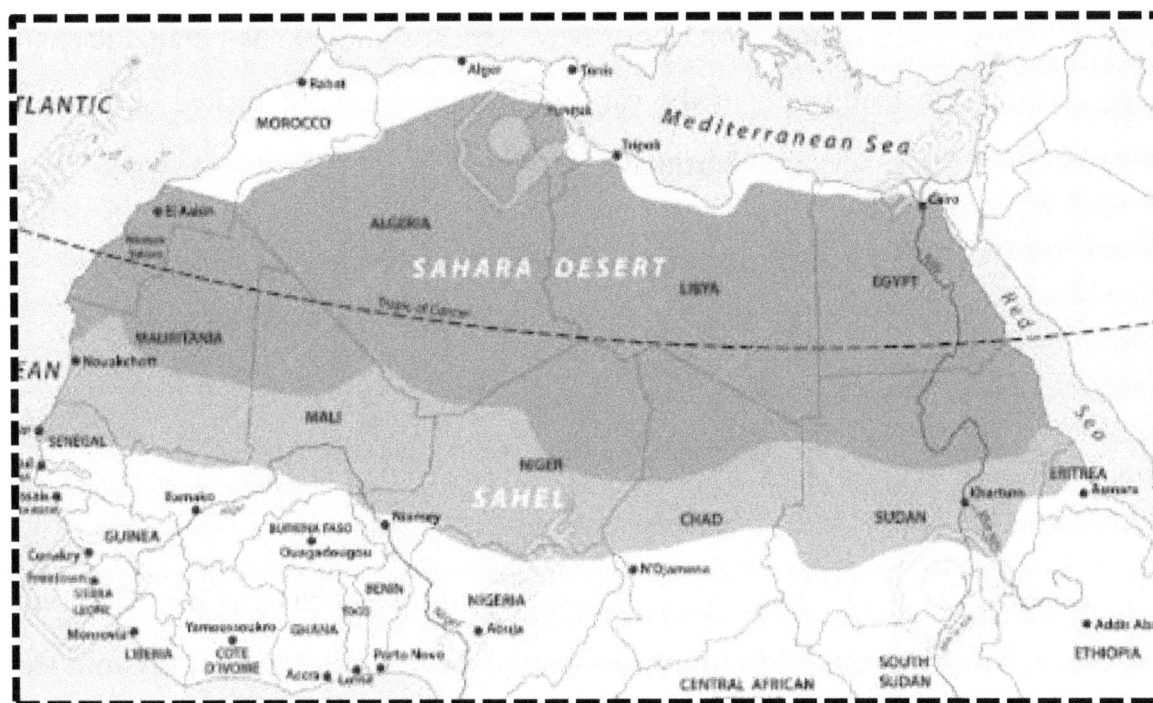

throughout the wider Sahara area, specifically in west and central Africa, an area termed by the Arabs as the Sudan "Land of the Blacks." (It was during the middle 20th Century that the country in central east Africa was officially labeled *Sudan*.) The Sahara was vast and bountiful, described as "a land of lakes, rivers, forests, green fields, villages, towns and cities."[41] It was also a connector to the rest of Africa north and south—a crossroads for trade across and through Africa. This region, over many centuries, eventually became a desert region covering three million square miles yet is certain to have lying beneath it many treasure-filled, lost civilizations. The Sahara continues to expand annually.

---

[41] Williams, C. 1974. *The destruction of black civilization.* p. 195.

Beginning in the 15th Century, European white "scholars" used the steady encroachment of the desert as a tool to delineate what became known as north Africa and "below the Sahara" Black Africa; another effort to de-Blacken northern Africa's history. The physical complexion of northern Africans underwent a dramatic change largely during the campaigns of the various European nations related to the trans-Atlantic slave trade. Says Van Sertima[42]:

> *The inhabitants of present-day North Africa are considered ethnically and culturally distinct from the people dwelling south of the Sahara. This is only so today because of the considerable influx of European types during the white slave trade and their later movement in positions of dominance after the defeat of the Moors.* (which occurred around 1492 a.d.)

North Africa was eventually home to other groups, including brown Asiatics especially following the 7th Century beginning (then spread) of Islam. Some from coastal Europe, including the Greeks and Romans, had arrived before the beginning of the Christian era to study in Egypt's Mystery Temples and then for conquest in parts of northern Africa. Many indigenous Africans remained in northern Africa, while others seized the opportunity to move into other parts of Africa. They took their skills south of the Sahara. There they continued developing their own unique cultures, religion, military, universities, and more.

The Moors ("Blacks") of northwest Africa. Among the empires that were developed by Africans traveling directly west from the Nile Valley was the Moorish (Moor means "Black") civilization. The Moors greatly influenced southwest

---

[42] Van Sertima, I. 1991. *The golden age of the Moor.* New Brunswick Publishers, p. 4.

Europe's exposure to high levels of modern living in stark contrast to the rest of Europe. The Moors (residing in much of modern-day Morocco and Mauritania in western Africa) were just a short voyage by boat to Spain and Portugal. These Iberian Peninsula Europeans benefited from the Moors' advancements. (See modern map below of Europe's Iberian Peninsula and its proximity to northwest Africa). The

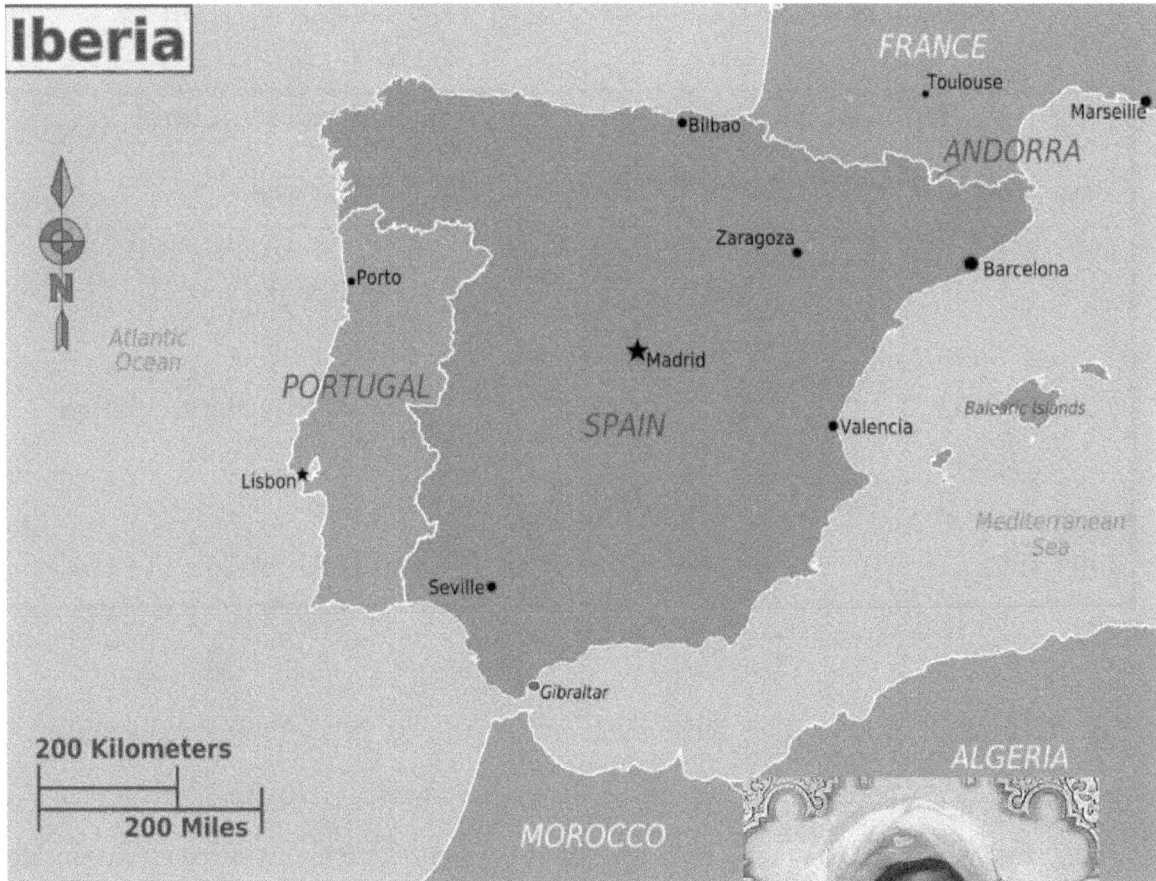

Moors exposed Europe to progressive thinking by opening universities throughout the region. This advanced their knowledge of science, mathematics, map-making, agriculture, architecture, art, and music. The Black Moors established western European cities and towns while most of Europe languished in

desperation, disease and chaos. A deeper study of the Moorish Empire, including delving into the brilliant military conquest of Spain and other victories under the leadership of **African General Tarik** (see photo representation above), can be found by examining, among others, Ivan Van Sertima's book, *Golden Age of the Moor* (1991).

West African Golden Age: The Major Empires

Three Major West African Empires General Timeline		
Approximate Years	*Empire/Event*	*Key figures*
300-1240 a.d. ?	Ghana (Wagadou)	Kaya Maghan (early monarch)?
1240 – 1645 a.d.	Mali	Mansa Sundiata, Mansa Musa
1464-1591 a.d.	Songhai	Sonni Ali, Askia the Great

The Ghana Empire. The westward expansion of Nile Valley civilization also features ancient Ghana as one of the earliest western African civilizations. The Ghana Empire is one of the better documented west African empires (though details of its extraordinary history remain tragically meager). The outstanding achievements of the Ghana Empire offer another case study validating Africans were not dependent upon whites to produce greatness.

The Empire of Ghana ("Ghana" is a title which means "leader" or "king"), or Wagadou, as it was called by the indigenous people, was situated in a swath of west

Africa slightly north and west of what is known today as the country of Ghana. The ancient empire was located in parts of the *contemporary countries of Mauritania, Senegal, and Mali*—an area that was referred to as **"Land of Gold."**

Ancient Ghana is the earliest of the documented empires, under the name of what is called the *Golden Age of West Africa*. It is believed to have reached a high level of cultural and scientific sophistication by 300 a.d., and some report it lasted for at least 1200 years. Chancellor Williams'[43] believed it was prominent even further back in antiquity, noting:

> *Ghana's actual history goes far back beyond its known record. That record listed forty-four kings before the Christian era, and this alone would extend Ghana's known history beyond the 25th Dynasty when the last black pharaohs ruled Egypt (7th century b.c.)*. P. 210

Ghana's architectural expertise was one indicator of its sophistication. Evidence shows the people had constructed many public buildings, canals, and irrigation systems. The greatest source of wealth, though, came from the empire's rich mineral resources mined, traded and controlled. Trading among Africans and neighboring groups had been transpiring cross-continentally—from East to West, from northern Africa to the Sudan. Among Ghana's coveted resources were gold, iron, and copper. Because of the advanced weapons and tools the people forged from the iron they mined, they gained dominion over the trade routes and acquired great wealth through taxation from the trade.

---

[43] Williams, C. 1974. *The destruction of black civilization.*

The ancient empire's capital city, Kumbi Saleh (located in modern-day southern Mali) was a central site for trade. Trading also afforded the various groups involved a way for ideas and innovations to be exchanged and further developed.

The people of ancient Ghana were a conquering people; they expanded the empire because they had one of the best military units, employing swords and lances. They were fierce, powerful, rich, and growing; so, simultaneously they became a target for others, who aggressively attacked them in pursuit of power and control over these lands and their destinies.

After centuries of wealth and control, Ghana was weakened by a group from northwestern Africa, the Almoravids, at some point during the late 11th century a.d. Ghana eventually splintered and fell. *"After the break-up of the Ghanaian Empire by invasions from many tribes, Ghana split apart into a number of states."*[44] After the decline,

---

[44] Windsor, R.. 1969. *From Babylon to Timbuktu*, p. 95

groups declared their independence, one of which was the Mandingos, who established the next great West African Empire, Mali in 1240 a.d.

It is worth noting that much later, at the close of European colonialism, an area named by the British colonizers as the British Gold Coast, was renamed "Ghana" by the indigenous people; done so as a memorial to the history and accomplishments of the ancient Ghana Empire. This re-naming occurred under **Kwame Nkrumah**, who in 1957, led this area to be the first west African country to regain independence from the invading white colonizers.

Golden Age of West Africa: Mali Empire. Mali is the second of the prominent west African Golden Age empires. It incorporated the Ghana Empire as it receded in power and stature. Mali comes from a word used by its people, the Mandingo, that means "free." Mali was established around 1240 a.d. when Mandingo King ("Mansa") Sundiata Keita defeated the Almoravids, the group that previously captured Ghana. He subsequently seized control over nearby territories and the salt and gold trade routes. **Sundiata was called "Lion King of Mali."**

Through his dealings with Muslim merchants, Sundiata converted to Islam (while maintaining indigenous practices), which had become a force to be reckoned with by this time. Many Africans converted to Islam, many others maintained indigenous religious practices tied to their culture and ancestry, and still others found it expedient to blend the two. White Christian "missionary" campaigns had not yet reached western Africa during the Golden Age. (That would come later when Europeans sought to exploit Africa's resources.)

Mali was expansive. At its height, the empire was occupied by 20 million people in 400 cities and towns. Its army included 100,000 men. Imagine the powerful, beautiful sight of this massive Black military! **No empire exceeded the size and stature of Mali except for the Mongols in China.** Europeans, at this time, were inconsequential. This is critical to understand how during Europe's Middle "Dark" Ages, a nothing-to lose-and-everything-to-gain mindset began to set in among Europeans who would soon usher in a campaign of theft of west Africa's resources and brutal human destruction through slave trading.

Mali extended out from Gao, on the Niger River in the central Sahara region and the empire stretched westward to the Atlantic coast. It included parts of the countries that are today called *Mali, Niger, Senegal, Mauritania, Burkina Faso, Nigeria, Guinea, the Gambia, and Chad.*

The Mali Empire was the first to establish Timbuktu as an international intellectual center, with the University of Sankore as a centerpiece. Sankore was recognized as a world-renowned university with instruction in theology, law, medicine, history, philosophy, astronomy and more. [45] **Gao, Jenne and Timbuktu** were the major trade cities and bustling urban centers of cultural and intellectual exchange. Mali was recognized for the people's love of justice and a high level of safety in the empire. Muslim scholar Ibn Battuta, when visiting in 1352 recorded[46]:

> *They are seldom unjust and have a greater abhorrence of injustice than any other people. Their sultan shows no mercy to anyone who is guilty of the least act of it. There is complete security in their country. Neither traveler nor inhabitant in it has anything to fear from robbers or men of violence.*

Besides Mansa Sundiata, one of Mali's most famed leaders was **Mansa Musa** (Mansa means "King" in the Mandinke language). King Sundiata was known for his intelligence and military strategy. His grand-nephew Mansa Musa (who came to power in 1307 a.d.) was lauded as one of the richest men in the world and the largest producer of gold. He was also the builder of many of the kingdom's great monuments, palaces, mosques and schools (Sankore was built under Mansa Musa's rule). Mansa Musa also formalized the relationship with the Muslim world by converting to Islam following a personal pilgrimage to Mecca during 1324 and 1325. The pilgrimage is said to have been massive including gold, fine jewels, human cargo,

---

[45] Windsor, R. *Babylon to Timbuktu.* p. 97
[46] Bovill, E. W. 1968. *The golden trade of the Moors* (2 ed.). Oxford: Oxford University Press. p. 95.

camels, and, it is said he spread so much gold along the way that the economies in the Mediterranean were overwhelmed.

Mali eventually weakened partly due to internal issues related to succession following Mansa Musa (whose date of death is not known for certain) and as smaller states saw the chance to break away. Among these were the Jolof (Wolof) people of modern-day Senegal who broke away in 1350 a.d. to establish an independent empire. Then a group of desert nomads seized Timbuktu, the richest city of the Mali Empire.

The greatness, power and breadth of Songhai surpassed that of both Ghana and Mali.

Simultaneously the Songhai nation began to rise from a smaller kingdom to an empire. Songhai and other smaller west African nations rose as Mali faded as a great West African empire.

Golden Age of West Africa: Songhai Empire. The Songhai Empire, considered the third of three Golden Age empires, held territory that was previously a part of the Mali Empire. Songhai rose to a high cultural, educational, and political level. Its beginning was around 1464 a.d. with **Sonni Ali Ber** who led military campaigns to grow Songhai's span of control from a kingdom (in a region previously a part of ancient Ghana) to an empire. **Sonni Ali** reigned as the Empire's first king until his death in 1492 a.d., and conquered major Mali trade cities including Jenne and Timbuktu (in 1468 a.d.). As a rising force, Songhai's highly effective military took control over the trans Saharan trade routes and thereafter experienced a steady expansion of both territory and wealth.

The greatness, power and breadth of Songhai surpassed that of both Ghana and Mali. Songhay covered a vast territory which is often noted as being larger than Europe

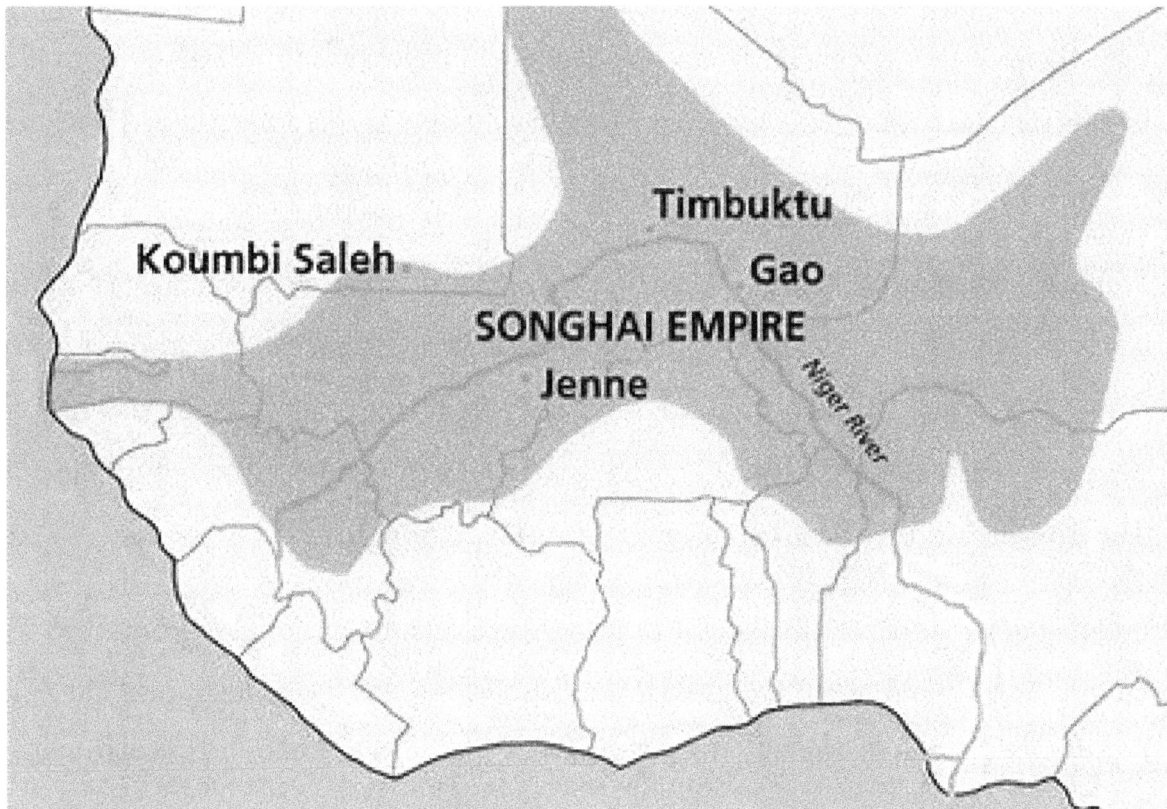

and engulfing much of West Africa. Its center was in what is today Mali along the River Niger; the empire extended in all directions from modern-day Senegal and Gambia eastward to include central Niger and northwest Nigeria.

To better support the trade business, Songhai was known for its sophisticated banking and credit system. **Askia the Great**, one of Songhai's greatest leaders (from 1493 to his 1528 death), expanded the educational centers throughout the empire, including Gao (the Empire's capital city), Jenne and Walata. These were in addition to the highly regarded University of Sankore, where people from around the world traveled for higher learning. Students were exposed to the latest thinking and innovations including in law and surgical procedures. Sankore housed over 700,000 manuscripts and laid the foundation for modern medical knowledge. Massive libraries, orchestral concerts, and the finest jewelry were commonplace in Songhai. Cites Lerone Bennett in *Before the Mayflower*, Timbuktu, during Askia's reign was an intellectual paradise. [47] Askia the Great's achievements kindled the influx of scholars and experts from across northern Africa, Asia, and Muslim Spain.

Songhai experienced many years of peace, cultural, intellectual and economic advancement until civil war erupted. Their northern Moroccan neighbors vied for control over the trade routes and succeeded in taking control over the Empire. Managing from afar, they found it not worth the effort to keep control over the gold. The Muslim Moors withdrew from the diminished Songhai Empire in 1661.

Songhai never re-established itself as a powerful empire, although it continued as a nation. The Empire fractured and weakened. During the Songhai Empire, the trade in humans expanded, initially through the capture of those who lost in battle; later they traded humans to supply labor to other countries. Much later, in 1901 the French colonial invaders conquered the old empire, doing everything to stamp out the memory of Songhai's greatness.

Other West African Kingdoms as Europeans Arrive

These three Golden Age Empires called Ghana, Mali, and Songhai, were not the only great west African nations before the onslaught of the Europeans. In this same region of West Africa and beyond, many other sophisticated African kingdoms flourished before and as desperate Europeans began their excursions into Africa's

---

[47] Bennett, L. 2016 edition. *Before the Mayflower*. P.19.

interior. These kingdoms also were envied by the Europeans who were immersed in and seeking a way out of the Dark Ages during the 15th Century a.d. **Kanem-Bornu** (east of Songhai), **the Hausa States** (with Kano as one of its most powerful states), and **Wolof Kingdom** (Coastal West Africa, today Senegal) are but a few of them. (See map below which includes some of these kingdoms). These cultures built on the accomplishments of their nearby African neighbors. All of these kingdoms were rich

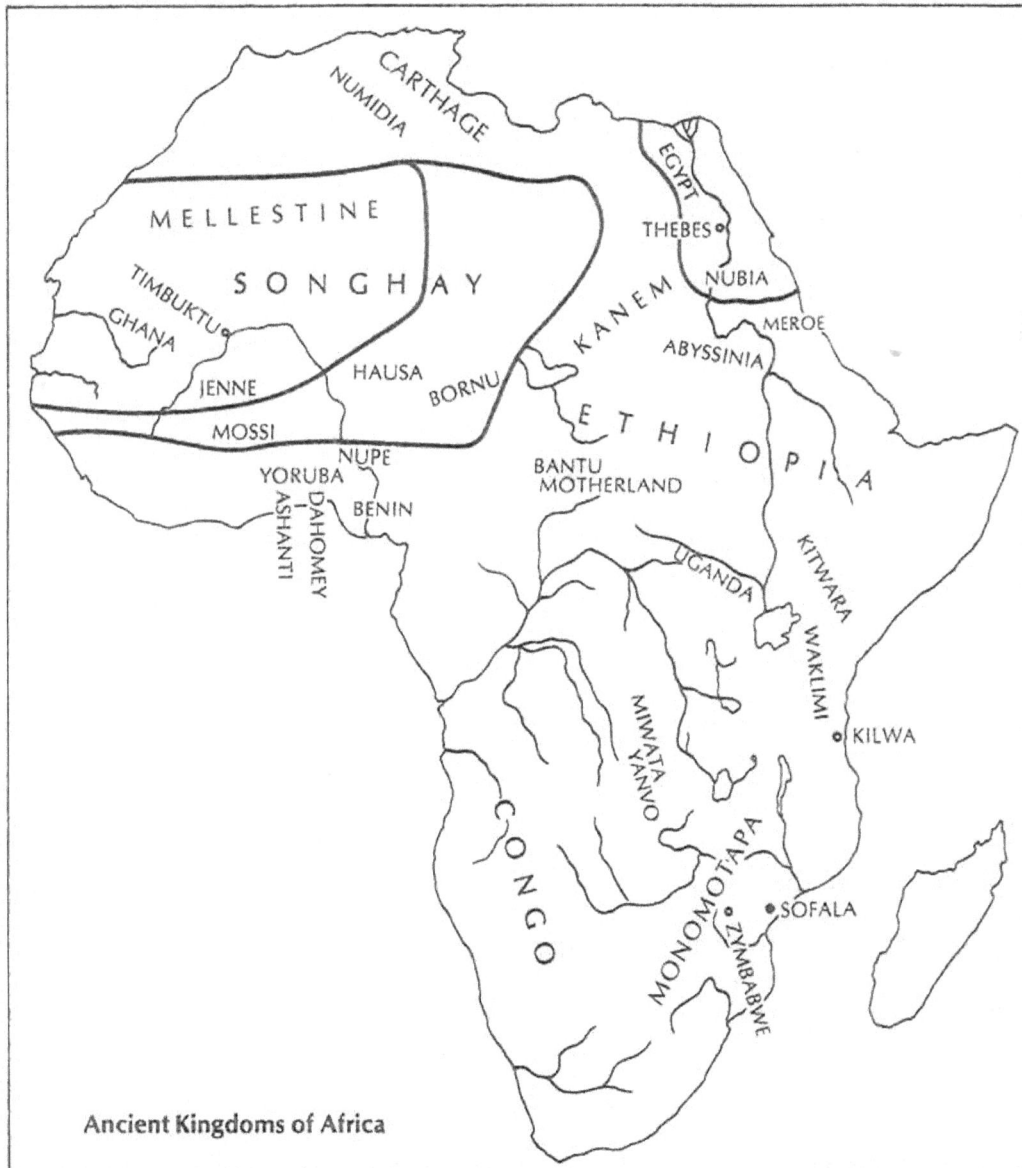

Ancient Kingdoms of Africa

in mineral resources, providing a base from which to build wealth and advance their cultures and scientific progress.

Kanem-Bornu was an empire that merged what was two separate kingdoms, Kanem (to the north) and Bornu (further south). Both were situated in parts of today's *Niger, Chad, Cameroon, and Nigeria.* They were famed for their iron technology and the use of horses for warfare. These nations were also known for their dominance over the trans-Saharan trade routes.

Empires proliferated in western Africa thanks to the mineral richness of the land, proximity to abundant sources of water and trade routes, and access to institutions of higher learning. **Oyo, Benin, Ashanti, and Yoruba** were a few other empires worth studying and provide further history to obliterate the white myth of "primitive Africa" before the white man came. Many of our brothers and sisters who've come to America for education or other reasons, can tell you which of these areas of west Africa they are from; they are able to plant their identity in one of these kingdoms— "I'm Yoruba", "My Baba is Ibo." etc. Those of us who came to America by way of the stench-filled slave ships have a hard time knowing exactly which nation holds our roots. What we are fairly certain about is that we are west Africans; thus, we hail from greatness. It is in our genes and part of the foundation of our identity.

Know that it was the richness in gold that first attracted the attention of the Portuguese, who initiated the European campaign of dominance in Africa. A few additional sources to expand your study of Africa before the Europeans arrived are:

- *West Africa Before the Colonial Era, Basil Davidson*
- *How Europe Underdeveloped Africa, Walter Rodney*

In Action: SECTION 7

1. What are two things you know now about the Golden Age of West Africa that you did not know before?

    a.

    b.

2. What were some of the resources of Africa that allowed kingdoms to develop to a high level?

    _____

    _____

    _____

3. Name five current countries in west Africa where great kingdoms flourished up through 1500 a.d.

    _____   _____

    _____   _____

    _____   _____

Section **8**

AFRICA

Europe's Violent Rise in Africa

Highlights:

1. Europe's destruction, theft and rape of Africa
2. Ongoing campaign to diminish Black identity
3. Closing thoughts

Sankofa bird
It is not wrong to go
back for that which you
have forgotten

Words Worth Heeding: *To a very great extent the problem with the education of black children, the crack epidemic and all of these other things we complain about day in and day out, are the result of a psychology that flows from a particular type of historical perspective.* —Amos Wilson

The slave trade became the means for Europe to rise from its Dark Age; the subsequent Partition of Africa and other tactics were used to sustain white supremacy.

Check out your mind

1. What was one major area in Africa where Europeans carried out the transatlantic slave trade?_____

2. What were two tactics white slave traders used to turn captured Africans into "slaves"?

   _____

   _____

3. What are two vicious strategies that white western nations used to steal long-term control over Africa?

   _____

   _____

While north and west African nations were increasing in both prosperity and sophistication, Europe was not so fortunate. By way of Egypt, the Greeks (then Romans) had for centuries borrowed and adapted Africa's art, culture, religious ideas, philosophy, architecture and more. These two European groups (Greeks and Romans) were considered, for centuries, to be the centers of European enlightenment, while the other more northern Europeans languished in barbarism.

Rome entered a period of decline, caused by internal and external factors. It officially fell in 476 a.d. This began the western Europe Dark Age, historically recorded as lasting nearly 1,000 years between the 5th and 15th Century a.d. (some mark its end as the 10th Century). It was characterized by a figurative "deep darkness"—evidenced by cultural deterioration, religious corruption, financial weakness, intellectual backwardness, disease and plagues, extreme violence, and barbarism. All the enlightened African practices the Romans learned from the Greeks, who had sat at the feet of Egypt's scholars, were but a memory. (Note that Rome overthrew the Greeks in 146 b.c. and became the dominant European nation at that time.)

> **Europe's Dark Age was characterized by a figurative "deep darkness"—with cultural deterioration, religious corruption, financial weakness, intellectual backwardness, disease and plagues, extreme violence, and barbarism.**

During the Dark Ages, disease was widespread. **Between 1350 and 1400 a.d., for example, the bubonic plague killed tens of millions, more than a third of Europe's population.** Western Europe suffered far worse conditions than eastern Europe (the eastern Roman Empire had relocated its capital from Rome to Constantinople). Led by the Byzantines, this part of Europe maintained more semblance of structure and stability through the middle of the 15th Century. Unsurprisingly, the western Europeans were desperate to gain some stake and control for themselves. Far western Europe was dominated by Islam, through its conquests after the religion was established around the 7th Century a.d. While Muslims were conquerors, they also played a role in bringing some level of cultural advancement to far western Europe's Iberian Peninsula as noted earlier (greatly influenced by their engagement with the African Moors). Nonetheless, the misery of most of western Europe seemed endless.

Some Key Events in Western Europe Prior to the Slave Trade	
476 .a.d.	Fall of the Roman Empire (in the west) marks beginning of European Dark Ages; the "eastern" empire is centered in Constantinople (lasted until 1453 a.d. while western Europe languished for centuries.)
711 a.d.	Spread of Islam, conquest of western Europe, and introduction of some civilized systems
1096-1291 a.d.	"Christian" crusades to recapture Rome (the "Holy Land") from Islam
1300 – 1475 a.d.	• Hundred-year war between England and France over land control • Bubonic plague, called "Black Death," wipes out 1/3 of Europe's population
1453 a.d.	Fall of Byzantine Empire in eastern Europe by Turks
1400-1492 a.d.	The Portuguese, the first Europeans to begin penetration in west Africa seeking gold and other trading commodities, established a trading post near Mauritania by 1445; began enslaving Africans; built Elmina Castle in 1481 a.d.

Was there human captivity before the transatlantic slave trade? There is no question about it. Enslaving humans had been a worldwide practice long before the beginning of the slave trade in west Africa. Whether it was as a condition for those captured in war, serfdom, debt bondage, or as part of an established class system, humans have found themselves subject to others. We should not be confused however in thinking these forms of enslavement and the trans-Atlantic trade were the same. *These other forms were never established as permanent life stations*, supported by legislation and religious doctrine that denied all rights and privileges based on race and affecting the entire race. Africans were involved as collaborators in the trade of tribal neighbors with whom they were warring. It is also known that many were bribed with gifts in exchange for surrendering their neighbors to slave mongers. **Yet, the nature of slavery once Europeans were involved, was unlike anything ever known.** There is likely no other time in human history that an entire institutional system, determined to steal wealth from others, invested so much into proving the rightness of their inexplicable wrong.

These other forms of slavery were never established as permanent life stations, supported by legislation and religious doctrine that denied all rights and privileges based on race and affecting the entire race.

Juxtaposing Europe's dismal, squalid history with that of west Africa's is critical to understanding the "why?" of the ruthless, devastation wreaked upon Africa. Europe's desperation to rise out of its Dark (Middle) Ages fueled their unrelenting assault on the lands and riches, namely west Africa, parts of Asia and the Americas. All of these areas had already been populated and civilized by various brown and Black people. (For more on African civilizations in the Americas, see these three books by Ivan Van Sertima's *They Came Before Columbus, African Presence in Early America*, and *African Presence in Early Asia*.)

Coastal areas of Africa- Gold Coast, Senegambia Coast. The Portuguese were first white nation to wage campaigns of conquest outside of Europe; they were desperate for resources to gain some semblance of progress. They took advantage of their contact with the African Moors from whom they learned and with whom they engaged in maritime trading. Traveling by water directly south of Portugal to the nearby African islands of Comoros and Cape Verde, they eventually made their way to the west African coast. Other European nations joined them, and they began to lead violent crusades throughout the rest of the glorious Continent.

> **Wherever we find ourselves today, wherever white power reigns supreme (largely in Europe and the Americas), remind yourself, these nations were built on the backs and talents of our forebears. We built them!**

The **four major players** in the enslavement of Africans and the decimation of west Africa's culture were **Portugal, France, Spain, and England**. Today's white world powers that built their nations' economic strength on the ruthless exploitation of Black slave labor over several centuries included those four plus **The United States and the Netherlands.**

Wherever we find ourselves today, wherever white power reigns (largely in Europe and the Americas), we should remind ourselves, these nations were built on the backs of our forebears. We built these nations. They did not have the capacity to build their own nations; instead, they brutalized us and plundered our homeland to access our skills without us ever being compensated even to this day. This is a reminder of our greatness and makes the case for reparations more than reasonable even if the chance of securing these repairs are slim.

(See below[48] the major areas along the west African coastline where ruthless European nations carried out their rape of Africa's human and mineral resources. Disregard the numbers as these tend to be far less than the actual lives lost.)

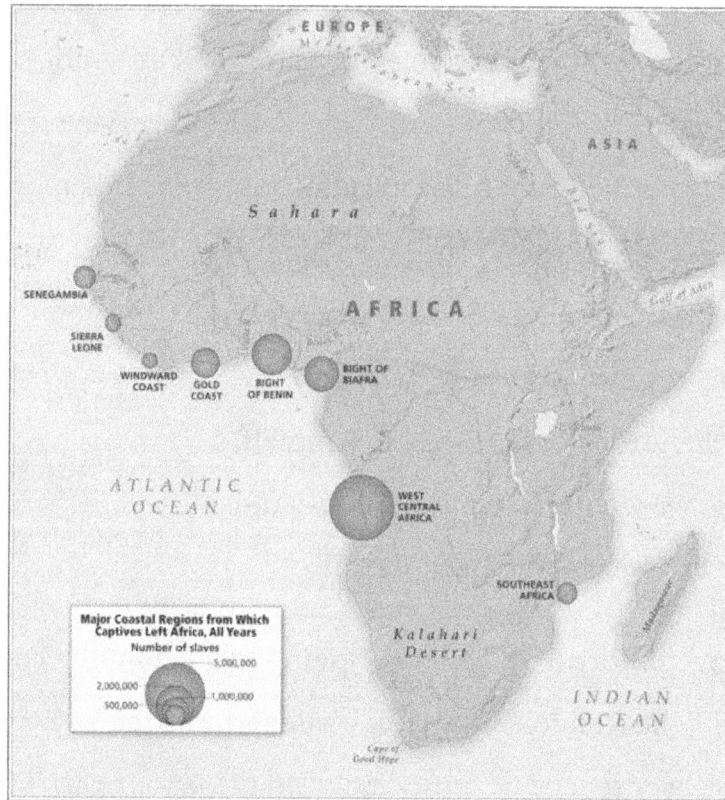

Note estimates of enslaved Africans by region/ country: Senegambia (Senegal and Gambia) 4.8%, Upper Guinea (Guinea, Guinea-Bissau and Sierra Leone) 4.1%, Windward Coast (Liberia and Cote d'Ivoire) 1.8%, Gold Coast (Ghana and east of Cote d'Ivoire) 10.4%, Bight of Benin (Togo, Benin and Nigeria west of the Niger Delta) 20.2%, Bight of Biafra (Nigeria east of Niger Delta, Cameroon, Equatorial Guinea, and Gabon) 14.6%, West Central Africa (Dem. Republic of Congo and Angola) 39.4%, Southeastern Africa (Mozambique and Madasgascar) 4.7%

---

[48] Source: Slavevoyages.com.

We are One People—scattered around the world. Estimates range widely about the number of Africans who were casualties of the transatlantic human bondage. Some say 12 million, others believe there were far more, up to 150 million! (The graphic below gives a glimpse of where our long-separated brothers and sisters, grandmothers and grandfathers, generations of our family members are.) This

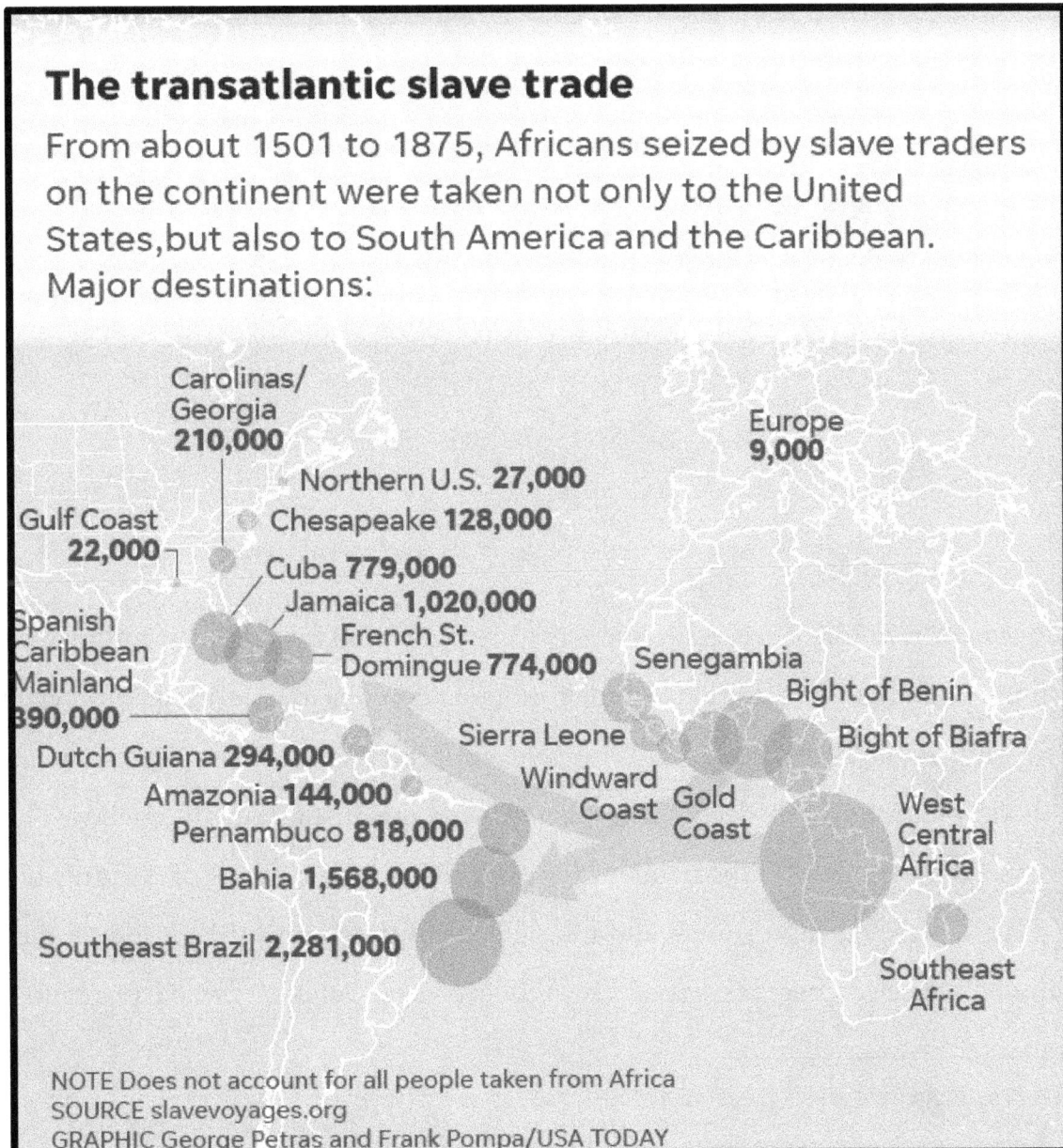

The transatlantic slave trade

From about 1501 to 1875, Africans seized by slave traders on the continent were taken not only to the United States, but also to South America and the Caribbean. Major destinations:

Carolinas/
Georgia
210,000

Europe
9,000

Northern U.S. **27,000**

Gulf Coast
22,000

Chesapeake **128,000**

Spanish
Caribbean
Mainland
390,000

Cuba **779,000**

Jamaica **1,020,000**

French St.
Domingue **774,000**

Senegambia

Bight of Benin

Bight of Biafra

Dutch Guiana **294,000**

Sierra Leone

Amazonia **144,000**

Windward
Coast

Gold
Coast

West
Central
Africa

Pernambuco **818,000**

Bahia **1,568,000**

Southeast Brazil **2,281,000**

Southeast
Africa

NOTE Does not account for all people taken from Africa
SOURCE slavevoyages.org
GRAPHIC George Petras and Frank Pompa/USA TODAY

holocaust impacted all of our people who were and are spread throughout the world. Tragically, we may never know how many of our people's lives were lost in this genocidal trade in human bodies. It is important for us to know we have kinspeople everywhere; the survivors are *our people* wherever they are.

Says Henry Louis Gates about the number of Africans arriving in the Americas:[49]

> *The most comprehensive analysis of shipping records over the course of the slave trade is the Trans-Atlantic Slave Trade Database. While the editors are careful to say that all their figures are estimates, they are the proverbial gold standard in the study of the slave trade. According to the database, between 1525 and 1866, 12.5 million Africans were shipped to the New World. Some 10.7 million survived the dreaded Middle Passage, disembarking in North America, the Caribbean, and South America. And how many of these 10.7 million Africans were shipped directly to North America? Only about 388,000. P. 9*

Religious rationale: The European enslavers were supported by academic and religious institutions in their justification for their inhumane practices, declaring and divinely bestowing upon Black bodies a God-given inferior status. Both Protestant and Catholic churches were deeply intertwined with the institution of slavery. They christened slave ships "in the name of Jesus" within which millions of Africans died of disease, were raped, tortured, and murdered. Others committed suicide on these "unholy" vessels. Churches, especially Anglican and Catholic, owned plantations.

---

[49] Gates Jr., L. 2017. *100 Amazing facts about the Negro. Kindle Edition.*

Their liturgy was forced upon enslaved Blacks who were taught the "righteousness" of obedience to slavery.

Academic rationale: White academia supported the slave trading enterprise by publishing treatises "proving" the "innate" inferiority of Blacks, including their claim that Blacks had small inferior brains when compared to whites. The book *Race, the History of an Idea in America*[50] illuminates the efforts of white "scholars" to prove the inferiority of Black people. Their work was one element in the white enslavers' justification for the enslavement, torture, and inhumane treatment of Black people. A few excerpts among many follow. The author, Gossett, shares the 1799 writings of Dr. Charles White, an English physician:

> *Negroes, White argues, occupy a different 'station' on the chain from the whites. In his opinion, the Negro is an intermediate species between the white man and the ape. Their skulls are smaller in internal capacity. Their nerves are larger, and their brains are smaller. Their bodies exude an unpleasant odor, a characteristic which is accentuated in apes.* P. 48

Speaking about George L. Buffon, an alleged authority on natural history during the 18th Century, Gossett tells us that,

> *For Buffon, the white race is the norm… Buffon does mention the fact that travelers in Africa have found Negro tribes so primitive that they cannot count beyond the number three, and he is willing to concede that the Negro has 'little genius.'* P. 36

---

[50] Gossett, T. F., 1997. *Race, the history of an idea in America*, New York: Schocken Books

A third example of this declaration of Black biological inferiority comes from one of America's founding fathers, Thomas Jefferson. Gossett cites Jefferson's *Notes on Virginia* of 1786:

> *Jefferson 'set down his reasons for believing that the Negro is condemned by nature to an inferior status. Jefferson argues, first of all, that the Negro is ugly…In addition, the Negroes have a 'very strong and disagreeable odor'…It is the mental and moral characteristics of Negroes, however, which Jefferson cites as the most obvious proof of their inferiority… 'They are more ardent after their female; but love seems with them to be more an eager desire, than a tender delicate mixture of sentiment and sensation'…'In memory they are equal to the whites; in reason much inferior, in imagination they are dull, tasteless and anomalous'. P. 42*

During the chattel slave period, the white western world used the weight of all of its institutional systems to declare and reinforce the premise of the innate inferiority of Black people. The academic, religious, economic, legal, and political communities coalesced to deeply scar Black people worldwide. They were deliberate in their effort to create in both Black captives and themselves a psychology of white superiority. It remains ingrained to this day.

Ongoing Campaign to Diminish Black Identity

Process of psychological/identity devastation. Again, we might wonder how to account for the lingering oppression of Blacks in America today, where we find ourselves at the bottom of most of the adverse statistical measures. And, why in

Africa, do these same deleterious factors persist as well (related to health, economics, education, family structure, etc.)? A basic understanding of the process by which Black people adapted to a condition of abject slavery in the West and colonialism in Africa would be reason to reframe our thinking about the current condition of Black people throughout the Diaspora.

The trans-Atlantic enslavement of Africans by European nations was far more than physical, it was deeply psychological, deliberately trauma-inducing and intent on making "Black" an emblem of a permanent slave condition. The journey from our homeland across the Atlantic Ocean, which typically took between one to three months, was a harrowing, devastating voyage designed to destroy the will of the captured west Africans. The

> **The enslavement of Africans by European nations was far more than physical; it was deeply psychological, deliberately trauma-inducing and intent on making "Black" an emblem of a permanent slave condition.**

whole experience is unfathomable—that humans were subjected to months crowded on a filthy ship, with the rampant spread of smallpox and dysentery, broken familial ties, hunger, no chance to exercise, lying beside dead bodies, or left to rot in the lower bowels of the stench-filled ships. With little care for the loss of life, with up to 50% of those stolen never arriving in the Americas, John Hope Franklin reminds us: *"the slave trade was still one of the most important sources of European wealth in the seventeenth and eighteenth centuries."* [51] P. 37

---

[51] Franklin. J. H. 1998. *From slavery to freedom.*

Plantation ready: "Breaking" down healthy racial identity. The experience of physical bondage was as traumatic as the capture in Africa itself. The orchestrated process of "making a slave" meant that, according to general estimates, 50%-60% of our forebears lost their lives during the capture and horrific Atlantic crossing. Further, of those surviving the Atlantic crossing (Middle Passage), another 30% to 50 % of those reaching the Americas for "seasoning"—to "break" us from our humanity—lost their lives too[52]. Most of those who survived the genocidal journey across the Atlantic Ocean were taken to the Caribbean for "seasoning"—a conditioning process. This was a traumatic process used to diminish our view of ourselves and force us to adjust to this new norm as a permanent, second-class race, as white people's property.

Genocidal Losses: 50%-60% of our forebears lost their lives during the capture and horrific Atlantic crossing. Another 30%-50% died during the seasoning process in the Americas.

We must never forget, however, that **there was resistance**. It was pervasive—during the capture, on the ships, on the plantations, on auction blocks, everywhere. Africans fought their white and traitorous Black captors; some jumped from canoes and ships to die rather than be enslaved. Others organized the overthrow of slave ships and entire plantations. Then others used cunning to poison plantation owners and overseers, the arbiters of this terrible condition. Articles published by the slaveholders in the American south, shared in Kenneth Stammp's *The Peculiar Institution* made clear that **docility was not the reality of plantation life.**

---

[52] Stannard, D. 1993. *American holocaust.* Oxford University Press.

The white plantation owners complained that Blacks were an ongoing "troublesome property", and *required* constant assault, barbaric whippings, brutal slave catchers, mutilations, selling off of family members, and more because Black men and women never relinquished the human yearning for freedom. Kenneth Stampp shares remarks from an antebellum North Carolina white plantation owner:

> *…Slavery and Tyranny must go together and that there is no such thing as having an obedient and useful Slave without the painful exercise of undue and tyrannical authority.* P. 141

To diminish this resistance, the white slave owners developed a system for imbuing a "slave psychology", a mentality that viewed Blackness as a badge of worthlessness and shame. Being Black meant that our sources of strength and meaning were stripped away. Our family structures, indigenous religions, languages, and cultures were dismantled and most often entirely eradicated. Stampp outlines the damage inflicted on enslaved Africans in his aptly named chapter **"To Make Them Stand in Fear."**

> *A wise master did not take seriously the belief that Blacks [Negroes] were natural-born slaves. He knew better. He knew that Negroes freshly imported from Africa had to be broken into bondage; that each succeeding generation had to be carefully trained. This was no easy task, for the bondsman rarely submitted willingly, he rarely submitted completely. In most cases, there was no end to the need for control.* P. 144

This **conditioning process** used by plantation owners included five discrete goals, achieved through specific actions ranging from manipulation to extreme violence, pitting Blacks against each other, to outright murder. Stampp identified these five "slave making" goals as:

To Make Slaves Who Stand in Fear:

1. Establish and maintain strict discipline

2. Implant in the bondsmen themselves a consciousness of personal inferiority... *"they had to feel that African ancestry tainted them; that their color was a badge of degradation."* P. 145

3. Awe them with a sense of their master's enormous power

4. Persuade them to take an interest in the master's enterprise and to accept his standards of good conduct

5. Impress upon the bondsmen their helplessness, to create in them *"a habit of perfect dependence"* upon their masters.

Ongoing conditioning: Centuries of seasoning and a never-ending program to ensure each succeeding generation born into an enslaved condition, all but ensured an inescapable dwarfing of the Black psychology of human equality. This process of "making a slave" unfortunately prevails to this day (with contemporary institutional support). "Slave-making" did not stop on the plantation; after the end of legalized slavery, the Jim Crow laws, Black Codes, and exploitation of labor with sharecropping all worked in tandem to maintain in the minds of Black people a sense of being *less than*.

Fifty years after Emancipation, the Red Summer of 1919 made clear that whites cared little for legal equality (notwithstanding the passage of the 13th, 14th and 15th Amendments). That year, in cities across the south, hundreds of Black people were murdered, many hung from trees as a sport. (**The National Memorial for Peace and Justice**, opened in 2018 in Montgomery, AL is a breathtaking, painful memorial of the common practice of terrorizing Black people through public lynching.)

Post legalized slavery tactics to engrain white supremacy: The trans-Atlantic African enslavement enterprise was the economic engine on which white wealth was established globally. Physical and psychic devastation was the enduring price paid by Diasporan Africans during the chattel slave experience in the Americas. Yet even that was not enough. Our kinspeople remaining in Africa were reduced to their lowest level of human value as well, including through means such as colonialism, the white Christian missionary movement and neo-colonialism. Eventually, as slave trading was abated and outlawed, a new system was put in place on American plantations to ensure the slave system of white wealth-building continued. One aspect of this new system was breeding Black humans, dishonoring Black humanity to birth "new slaves."

The Berlin Conference and its tragic aftermath. At the close of legalized slavery, Europeans took aggressive moves to maintain dominion over Africa's resources. The Berlin Conference was held November 15, 1884 through Feb. 26, 1885 and partitioned Africa among European countries. Also called the "Scramble for Africa," this dealt a devastating blow to Africa, second only to the rape, murder and enslavement of millions. When the conference was convened, only the coastal regions of Africa were colonized (a strategy connected to the mostly coastal trans-Atlantic slave trade). The Europeans, greedy and desperate for the resources across the African continent, haggled for three months over which European country would stake its claim in which parts of the Continent. The conference not only divided the African nations and land among Europeans, says Kenyan author Patrick Gathara[53],

Key Terms

Colonialism: direct control of the government and production in one country by another country; includes settlers and military to keep control

Balkanization: dividing a region or state into smaller ones that are often hostile with one another

Neo-colonialism: indirect rule and process for maintaining colonizers' influence over the economics of a nation that has gained independence

Partition of Africa: invasion, occupation, division and colonization of Africa by European powers between 1884-1914

It did something much worse, with consequences that would reverberate across the years and be felt until today. It established the rules for conquest and partition of Africa, the process legitimizing the ideas of Africa as a playground for outsiders, its mineral wealth as a resource for the outside world not for Africans and its fate as a matter not to be left to Africans.

A total of 13 European countries and the United States gathered for the Berlin Conference in Berlin, Germany to rob Africa of its riches. **Not a single African was invited to the table!** Convened by the Germans, these oppressors attended and are signatories on the Berlin Act:

- Austria-Hungary
- Belgium
- Denmark
- France
- Germany
- Great Britain
- Italy
- The Netherlands
- Portugal
- Russia
- Spain
- Sweden-Norway
- Ottoman Empire
- United States

[53] Gathara, P. *Berlin 1884: Remembering the conference that divided Africa.* Nov. 15, 2019. Online access.

They authorized navigating further into the African interior (not just the coastal areas that had been ravaged for three centuries). These Europeans haggled for years, and some fought each other, before finalizing the Partition of Africa. Each was aiming to get as much of the prize as they could, to gain economic control of Africa's most bountiful regions. Their actions had devastating consequences for Africans. These European nations formalized (and reinforced through a new white hegemony that took precedence over existing governments) a new hodgepodge of 50 nations

African Colonization After the Berlin Conference (1884–1885)

with artificial boundaries without respect for the 1,000 existing indigenous nations. This fomented what would become lasting conflict and fratricidal hatred across African groups; they deliberately divided unified groups and merged groups that were in conflict.

The map on the previous page represents how Africa was carved up by the 13 European countries. **By 1914, Africa had been fully divided among Europeans into 50 countries with only Liberia and Ethiopia remaining as independent nations.**

We wonder today about the atrocities the Hutus and the Tutsis committed against each other; their conflicts, like many others were deliberately incited through the actions of the Berlin Conference. The reinforcement of these new boundaries required and included untold fratricidal massacres and white violence against Africans resisting the change.

> *The Berlin Conference was Africa's undoing in more ways than one.*
> *The colonial powers superimposed their domains on the African continent. By*
> *the time independence returned to Africa in 1950, the realm had acquired a*
> *legacy of political fragmentation that could neither be eliminated nor made to*
> *operate satisfactorily.* [54]

Late Tanzanian President Julius Nyerere, who sought reunification of the various indigenous groups, said:

---

[54] Harm J. deBli. Nov. 25, 2013. *Geography: Realism, regions and concepts.* Wiley. 16th edition.

We are artificial 'nations" carved out at the Berlin Conference in 1884, and today we are struggling to build these nations into stable units of human society…we are in danger of becoming the most Balkanised continent of the world.

Still We Rise. With the Balkanization of Africa, it is almost unfathomable that Black people across the Diaspora have the will and mind to still seek reclamation of our stolen, yet long-glorious identity. With meager access to opportunities, Black people continue rising around the globe. The African independence movement of the mid-60s, the Civil Rights and Black Power movements in the US are crucial starting points on our journey. These transformation Movements were part of the protracted struggle to reclaim our identity. The challenges are not only physical and political but more so, we must be determined to undo the ravages of the psychological identity destruction we have all suffered at the hands of a worldwide white oppressor. These Movements and subsequent achievements show us that once we know who we are, we know what we are capable of. As Maya Angelou told us, "Still we Rise" –breaking through barriers and restrictions to achieve at remarkable levels.

In Action: SECTION 8

1. Review the section on the five goals of the plantation seasoning process. How do you see any of these goals still being lived out today?

Which goal?	How is it alive today?

2. Write three ideas that you would share with someone who wanted to understand what happened between our greatness in Africa and our current situation with so many negative social outcomes?

_____

_____

_____

3. How would you explain the grand accomplishments of Black people today despite the many forces stacked against us in the U.S.?

Closing Thoughts:

What We Owe Ourselves and Our Children

As Black parents, teachers, mentors, and community leaders, we owe our children a chance for self-realization, to know just how capable they are. We believe that requires nurturing and reinforcing a healthy racial identity in all of them. This is our debt and gift to succeeding generations. Part of paying that debt is being unequivocal and unashamed in exposing them to the powerful Black stories and artifacts of our past and present that enable them to "know" they are *powerful beyond measure.*

The western world's invention of a history that asserted non-white racial inferiority had a primary purpose of leading Black people into a process of cultural genocide. As Black people began to adopt the erroneous version of history, we became ashamed of Africa and our African origins. Black skin became an emblem of self-contempt and a visible reminder of our race's inferiority. The conditioned self-hatred lead us to psychologically disconnect from Africa. We have been denied knowledge of an African-centered, scientifically validated culture, a culture which affirmed our innate human equality and potential. Black people identified with the culture of the white oppressor to escape the psychic pain associated with our African roots. Through identification Black people unconsciously accept the white dominant culture and its underlying belief in white supremacy and Black inferiority.

Calling ourselves African Americans is insufficient to reclaim our identity with our homeland and culture. To overcome cultural genocide and the racial neurosis it breeds, we must rediscover the genius of our African ancestors and the significant role they played in the development of human civilization and culture. We must insist on re-establishing the broken strand of continuity between our African history and our history of Africans in America. Ours is one historical narrative that was deliberately severed in America. With that, we must also see ourselves as responsible for the restoration and perpetuation of that great continuous legacy today.

The capacity for any group of people to function together productively for their common well-being is dependent on the nature of their historical consciousness. That is because personal and collective identity is an outgrowth of historical consciousness. As Black people, we have been victimized by an educational process that willfully disconnected us from the glories of our African past, our history prior to the slave trade. This deliberate historical discontinuity has been a source of a severe, unconscious memory loss, leading to a form of social amnesia and a pathological system-induced dementia. This dementia generates within our minds a distorted historical consciousness and a self-destructive personal and collective identity. The culprit is our miseducation.

By design, we do not know who we really are, all we really are. Sadly, we have become, in our own minds, who our oppressor has told us we are.

It has been said: *"The loss of memory is a loss of identity. If you cannot remember who you really are, you are at risk of becoming someone else."*

To know who we really are requires we heal our minds and restore racial memory. Knowledge of our

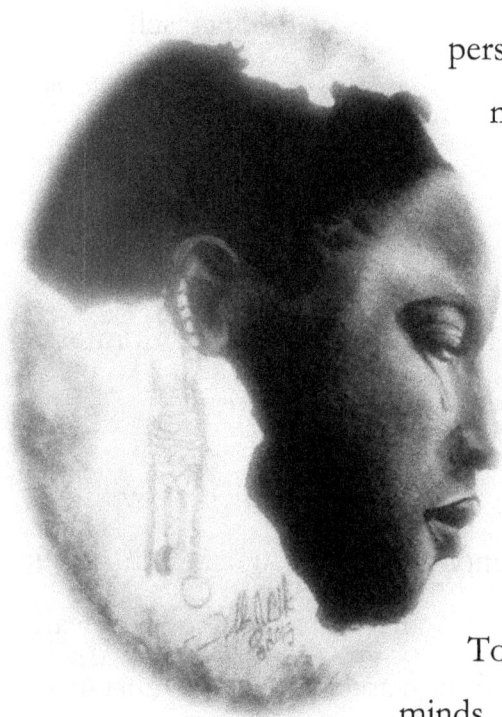

history enables us to stop our second-guessing and shrinking ourselves and our children to fit the second-class identity given to us. We must re-enliven the glories of our African past, the many achievements that did not rely upon whiteness or white approval. If we think about the unremitting efforts to destroy Black will and worth, it is remarkable we survived. We possess something special—an unparalleled resilience—upon which to build for the next generations.

Connections Remembered is meant to be a bridge to the history of Blacks in America, which is far better documented. The idea is that our children must never believe the plantation was our starting point. Restoring memory of our racially healthy identity grounded in stellar, hallmark accomplishments is key to what we believe are the possibilities today.

Connections Remembered is meant to help free our minds. It is a part of opening the minds, hearts and curiosity of Black people. We trust this encourages you to dig deeper into the history of our glory and our pain. Once we begin freeing our minds, we thrive. May the journey of self-discovery and reclamation continue.

Appendix

AFRICA

Highlights:

1. Glossary
2. Timeline of ancient African history
3. Reading and reference lists

Owo foro adobe
Performing the unusual
or the impossible.

Words Worth Heeding: *The discontents of individuals reflect the discontents of groups; and these, the discontents of the societies and cultures they constitute. The Great Chain of Discontents inextricably binds together individual, group, society, and culture.*

—**A**mos N. Wilson

Glossary

African Centered	A curricular perspective that views and centers human existence through the lens of humanity's African origins and the experiences of and impact on African people (both in Africa and the Diaspora). Inclusive of other groups, it ensures those of African descent receive their proper placement and others also understand their indebtedness to Africa.
Ankh	Kemetic symbol for life; it represents the union of the male and female principle and subsequent creation of a new existence.
Archaeologist	One who studies past human life by utilizing the remains of ancient people; these remains include tools, artifacts, and customs.
Book of the Dead	(Book of Coming Forth by Day)—a collection of ancient Kemetic texts that were originally written on papyrus and placed in the tombs of pharaohs. These writings include the Pyramid and Coffin texts.
Cataract	Fierce rapids formed by large rocks in several places along the Nile River. The Nile has six cataracts.
Coffin Text	Sacred writings written on the inside of the Tombs of Commoners.
Continental Drift	The slow movement of the earth's land masses, thought to be caused by shifting of the tectonic plates.
Dynasty	A period of rule by one or more families
Ethnocentrism	To teach that one group's cultural knowledge is the only "valid" cultural knowledge.
Eurocentric	To view knowledge from the false notion that Europe was the point of origin for humanity and civilization, and that its culture is superior to others.
Fault	In geology, a break in the earth's surface caused by the shifting of plates which form the mantle upon which the earth sits. Within the earth's faults lie ancient fossil remains.
Fossils	The hardened remains or traces of an animal, human or plant of a previous age, preserved in the earth's crust.

Geologist	A scientist who studies the earth's crust, the layers of which it is composed and their history; concerned with the age of rocks.
Giza	A city on the outskirts of Cairo, Egypt where the Great Sphinx and the Great Pyramids of Pharaohs Khufu, Khafre, and Menkaure are located.
Gondwanaland	The name ascribed to the southern and largest supercontinent, which came into existence about 200 million years ago. Africa was the center of this southern land mass. This mass included today's continents South America, Africa, and Antarctica and the large land masses known as Australia and India.
Hominids	Having to do with anyone belonging to the family of primate type (highest order of mammals), which includes humans. Humanity is the only existing hominid today.
Homo	Any of the class of primates comprising early and modern humans
Ice Age	Any of the times during which the earth was covered with glaciers; the most recent time was in Europe with estimates ranging between 50,000 and 20,000 years ago.
Kemet	The "land of the Blacks." The name used by the original inhabitants of Egypt for their nation.
Laurasia	The name ascribed to the northern supercontinent, which came into existence about 200 million years ago. It included what today is called North America, Europe and Asia (Eurasia).
Mammals	One of a class of animals that are warm-blooded, having a backbone and feed their young with mother's milk. Humans are part of this class.
Nubia	A region that originally extended from Southern Kemet (1st cataract) into what is today Northern Sudan (6th cataract) east to the Red Sea and west to Libya
Paleontologist	The scientist who studies early life forms, as represented through fossil remains of animals and plants. He/she is specifically interested in the organisms which caused the life forms.
Pangaea	"All land"; the idea that the earth was one land mass, rather than and before there were seven distinct continents, approximately 200-600 million years ago. This land mass was surrounded by a mass of water, referred to as Panthalassa ("All sea"). It is believed that this single land

	mass began to break up, forming two supercontinents approximately 200 million years ago.
Papyrus	A plant grown in the delta of Kemet that was used to make ropes, baskets, sandals, and paper. The paper made from papyrus was made into scrolls.
Pharaoh	Asian word for the Kemetic (Egyptian) kings.
Piltdown Man	A fossil forgery of an early human; found in England in 1912 and included bones of a human and an orangutan.
Pyramid Texts	Religious and philosophical writings recorded on the interior walls of the pyramids of Pharaohs Unas, Teti, and Pepi.
Pyramids	Royal tombs of Kemet
Saqqara	A city 15 miles south of present-day Cairo, Egypt; the location of a major temple complex and the Step Pyramid designed by Imhotep.
Sphinx	Statue that is usually comprised of the body of a lion and the head of a man or woman
Tectonic Plates	Major slab-like sections that make up the structure of the earth's crust; the number of these plates varies depending on the source; the range averages between six and nine major plates
Wa'Set	The original name of the Kemetic city that was called Thebes by the Greeks and Luxor by the Arabs.

Timeline of African Origins

(not all-inclusive)

20 billion years	**Origin of the Universe?**
4.6 billion years	Formation of the Earth
4.2 billion	Evidence of the first rocks
3.5 billion	First single-cell life in AFRICA, Swaziland
600 million years ago	Existence of Pangaea (AFRICA the center)
200 million years ago	Gondwanaland (from Gondwana gradual splitting) facilitates the spread of many life forms throughout the world's southern hemisphere (from the AFRICAN center)
12 million years	Probable age of first hominids—human ancestors (AFRICA)

Ca. 4.0 million years	All the homo family (began in AFRICA)
	
	• Australopithecus:
	    o (3.75 millions of years)—Laetoli, Tanzania, 1975 by Mary Leakey
	    o (3.0 million years)—Hadar, Ethiopia, 1979 by Don Johanson
	    o (1.75 million years Australopithecus Boisei)—Olduvai Gorge, Tanzania, 1959 by Mary and Louis Leakey
	• Homo habilis:
	    o (2.7 million years)—"1470 man", Lake Turkana, Kenya, 1972 by African Bernard Ngeneo (Leakey team member)
	• Homo erectus:
	    o (1.5 million years)—East Turkana, Kenya, 1975 by Leakey team member

130,000-200,000 years	Homo sapiens and Homo sapiens: Omo, Ethiopia; Laetoli, Tanzania; Klasies River Mouth and Border Cave, South Africa (takes primacy over Europe's Neanderthal)
60,000-100,000 years?	European Neanderthal Man fossils (proven recently to not be a part of the lineage to modern homo sapiens; see Martin Meredith); found in 1856, Neanderthal Valley, Germany
75.000 b.c.	Wurm Glacial period begins covering Europe and North America with one-mile inch thick sheet of ice
35,000-50,000 years?	European Cro-Magnon Man fossils, SW France, found in 1868
40,000-37,000 b.c.	Beginning practice of metallurgy (for tools and weapons); groups of African people were gathered in enough numbers to advance their communal, social and basic survival systems.
20,000 b.c.	Kemet (which had its origins in the south, i.e. Nubia) first began, though oral records indicate that a considerable amount of activity was taking place as early as 20,000 b.c.
10,000 – 6,000 b.c.	Dawn of the Agricultural Era in Africa, laying the foundations for the rise of renowned Africa civilizations (Egypt and Nubia)
4,100 b.c.	The rise of NUBIA, the oldest civilization Civilization was evident in various areas in the Nile Valley (Kush, Punt, Ethiopia, Sudan and Egypt). The Tasili rock painting demonstrate Black habitation of the Sahara back to at least 8,000 b.c.
3,100 b.c.	Unification of Egypt: The first Egyptian Dynasty; first Pharaoh of united Egypt (Narmer or Menes) is from south (Upper Egypt); writing had developed; the 365 ¼ day calendar was developed.
3,000 b.c.	The first great civilization of India was established by the Black Dravidians in the Indus Valley. They cultivated wheat and cotton, possessed boats and wheeled carts, domesticated animals, and were skilled workers in bronze and iron. They also built large cities, e.g., Mhenjo Daro and Harappa with main and side roads. The Minoans moved from northern Africa to Crete. The Minoan Civilization had its origins in Black North Africa.

2.800 b.c.	1st Golden Age/Pyramid Age; Imhotep builds Step Pyramid of Egypt
2,200 b.c.	2nd Golden Age/Middle Kingdom; Literary Age
1,500 b.c.	3rd Golden Age/New Kingdom; Temple and Imperial Age
332 b.c.	Alexander's Invasion (Greeks) and conquest of Egypt and all north Africa; First European onslaught on the culture and civilizations of Africa.
300 a.d. ?	Golden Age of West Africa begins with Ghana Empire, through 1240 ad
476 a.d.	Fall of Roman Empire, beginning of Europe's Dark Ages (through about end of 15th century)
711 a.d.	Spread of Islam, and conquest of western Europe and introduction of some civilized systems
1096-1291	"Christian" crusades to recapture Rome (the "Holy Land") from Islam
1300 – 1475 a.d.	Hundred-year war between England and France over land control Bubonic plague "Black Death" wipes out 1/3 of Europe's population
1400-1492 a.d.	The Portuguese, the first Europeans begin penetration in west Africa seeking gold and other trading commodities, established a trading post near Mauritania by 1445; began enslaving Africans; built Elmina Castle (1481 a.d.) Transatlantic Africa slave trade
1884-1914 a.d.	European Berlin Conference and Partition of Africa, the carving up of Africa, colonialism
1957 a.d.	First African nation, Ghana, gains independence under Kwame Nkrumah

References & Book List

indicates basic must-read books for students new to African history

*Ben-Jochannan, Y., 1981. Black man of the Nile. NY

_____. 1970. Africa: Mother of western civilization.

_____. 1970. African origins of the major western religions. NY: Alkebu-lan Books.

_____. 1969. Africa: The land, the people, the culture. NY: W.H. Sadlier, Inc.

Bennett, Jr., L.. 1962. Before the Mayflower. Chicago, Johnson Publishing.

Bernal, M. 1987. Black Athena, Volume I. New Brunswick, NJ, Rutgers University Press.

Bradley, M. 1978. Iceman inheritance. Kayode Publications Ltd.

*Browder, A. T. 1992. Nile Valley contributions to civilization. Washington, DC: Institute of Karmic Guidance.

Darwin, C. 1871. The descent of man, and the selection in relation to sex. London: J. Murray.

_____. 1859. On the origin of the species by means of natural selection. London: J. Murray.

Davidson, B. 1974. Africa in history. NY: Collier Books.

_____. 1998. West Africa before the colonial era. NY, Routledge.

Diop, C. A. 1981/1991. Civilization or barbarism: An authentic anthropology. Brooklyn, NY: Lawrence Hill Books.

*_____. 1974. The African origin of civilization: Myth or reality? NY: Lawrence Hill and Company.

DuBois, W. E. B. 1970. The education of Black people. Herbert Aptheker (ed.), NY: Monthly Review Press

*_____. 1965. The World and Africa. NY: International Publishers.

Fairchild, J. E. 1964. Principles of geology. NY: Holt, Rinehart, and Winston.

Finch III, C. S. 1991. Echoes of the old darkland: Themes from the African Eden. Decatur, GA: Khenti, Inc.

Franklin, J. H. & Moss, Jr. A. 1998. From slavery to freedom, sixth ed., McGraw Hill.

Higgins, G. 1836. Anacalypsis, attempt to draw aside the veil of Saitic Isis: an inquiry into origins, languages, nations, and religions, Vol. 1 and 2, London: Longman, Rees, Orme, Brown, Green and Longman, Pater, Noster Row.

Hilliard, A. Williams, L., and Damali, N. 1987. The teachings of Ptahhotep oldest book in the world. Atlanta, GA: Blackwood Press.

*Jackson, J. H. 1970. Introduction to African civilization. Secaucus, NJ: Citadel Press.

James, G. .M. 1954. Stolen legacy. San Francisco: Marcus Books.

Johanson, D., and Edey, M. 1981. Lucy: The beginnings of humankind. NY: Simon & Schuster.

Karenga, M. 1993. Introduction to Black studies. Los Angeles: The University of Sankore Press.

_____. Ed. 1989. Selections from the Husia—Sacred wisdom of ancient Egypt. Selected and retranslated, second printing. Los Angeles: University of Sankore Press.

King, L.C. 1983. Wandering continents and spreading sea-floors on an expanding earth. London: Wily? And Sons.

Kotkin, J. 1992. Tribes: How race, religion, and identity determine success in the new global economy. NY: Random House.

*Leakey, R. E. and Lewin, R. 1992. Origins revisited. NY: Doubleday.

_____. 1981. The making of mankind. NY: E. P. Dutton.

_____. 1977. Origins. NY: E. P. Dutton.

*Madhubuti, H. and Madhubuti, S. 1991. African centered education: Its value, importance, and necessity in the development of Black children. Chicago: Third World Press.

Maspero, G. 2015. History of Egypt, Vol. 1. CreateSpace Independent Publishing.

Massey, G. 1990. Ancient Egypt: The light of the world, Vol. 1 and 2. Reprint. NY: Eca Associates.

_____. 1881. Book of beginnings, Volume II.

O'Toole, T. 1977, November 16. "Seeds of life trace to African fossils." The Atlanta Journal Constitution. P. 14A

Petrie, W. M. F. 1939. The making of ancient Egypt. NY: Macmillan.

_____. 1903. A history of Egypt form the earliest times. London: Methuen & Company.

Rogers, J.A. 1961. Africa's gift to America. Middletown, CT, Wesleyan Press.

Schwarzbach, M. 1986. Alfred Wegener: The father of continental drift. WE: Science Tech, Inc.

Seabrook, C. 1977, March 24. Is man innately violent? Atlanta Journal, A3.

Sullivan, W. 1991. Continents in motion: The new Earth debate, 2nd ed. NY: American Institute of Physics.

Tarling, D. H. 1971. Continental drift: A study of the Earth's moving surface. London: G. Bell & Sons Ltd.

Van Sertima, I. 1993. Egypt revisited. New Brunswick, NJ: Transaction Publishers.

_____. 2003. They came before Columbus: The African presence in ancient America. Random House Publishing Group.

Villegas, A. M. 1988. School failure and cultural mismatch: Another view. Urban Review, 20:4, p. 253-265.

Wells, H. G. 1940. The outline of history. NY: Triangle Books.

*Williams, C. 1974. The destruction of Black civilization: Great issues of a race form 4500 b.c. to 2000 a.d. Chicago, IL: Third World Press.

Wilson, A. 1993. The falsification of Afrikan consciousness. NY: Afrikan World Infosystems.

About the Authors

Sondai and Lindiwe Lester have spent more than 35 years each in public sector leadership. Their vocation has been as liberation theologians at the Pan-African Orthodox Christian Church, followed by service in nonprofit leadership and human development consulting. All along, we have been researching, writing and teaching African and African American history to adults and youth. A source of great pride has been the mentoring relationships we have built across generations of young adults helping them develop their grounding in a strong, healthy racial identity.

For us, historical study is more than a nice pursuit. It is the foundation for tapping into our inner strength as a people to face and be a part of transforming the world. Black history has provided a framework and basis to explain the "why" of our past and current Black condition. It is part of the connective tissue that enabled Black folks' resilience and ingenuity down through the years, despite unthinkable oppression.

We raised our children and supported many families and friends through conversations about race, justice, and personal power. We hope we have planted seeds that continue growing the capacity of our people for self-determination and liberation. We know what *tribe* we belong to; we place it first, and we view the world through the prism of the implications for our tribe's empowerment and well-being.

Sondai has a Master of Arts in Reading, underwent doctoral studies in educational administration and attended seminary at Atlanta's Interdenominational Theological Center. He is President of P.S.E. Institute (Planting Seeds of Excellence) a consultancy for educational development and publishing. Lindiwe has Master of Education and Educational Specialist degrees. She also is a certified executive coach. Lindiwe retired as a nonprofit executive and is currently President of Tap In Coaching and Consulting.

Contact P.S.E. Institute for further conversations, additional books, seminars, educator development, etc.

lsondai@hotmail.com

lindiwe@tapinconsulting.com

Thank you for reading and joining us on the journey to reclaim healthy Black identity.